Reading
Writing
& Parents
Who Care

Reading Writing & Parents Who Care

John Koster

VICTOR BOOKS®

A DIVISION OF SCRIPTURE PRESS PUBLICATIONS INC.
USA CANADA ENGLAND

Library of Congress Cataloging-in-Publication Data

Koster, John P., 1945–
   Reading, writing, and parents who care / John P. Koster.
      p. cm.
   Includes bibliographical references.
   ISBN 0-89693-886-7
   1. Education, Elementary — United States — Parent
participation.
   2. Home and school — United States. 3. Christian education — United States. I. Title.
   LB1048.5.K67 1991
   649′.68 — dc20   91-7217
                                                        CIP

1 2 3 4 5 6 7 8 9 10 Printing/Year 95 94 93 92 91

Contents

Introduction

"OK, Emily! Attack!"

"Yah! Yah! Yah!"

Slashing with both hands, kicking with both wobbly legs, my five-year-old *ninja* girl ripped the paper bag to shreds as I swung it to simulate a five-year-old opponent.

"That's pretty good, Emily. Why don't you yell *'banzai'* when you attack?"

"Dad, that's silly."

"OK, maybe you're right. Let's do it one more time."

Emily had no interest in the martial arts. She was studying karate so she could attend kindergarten in a middle-class neighborhood without getting beaten up.

Suddenly it hit me. My daughter really didn't want to be a *ninja*. She wanted to be an opera singer. Why was I teaching a Christian child how to break people's windpipes or rupture their groins? The answer was: so she can sit around and catch colds without getting punched, while she listens to other kids recite the alphabet—even though she already knows how to read.

Public opinion collapsed in a shambles as reason finally broke through to me. Emily really didn't need school—and neither did I.

Emily had entered school full of bright hopes and sweet expressions three months earlier. She had faithfully watched "Mister Rogers," "Sesame Street," and "The Electric Company," and her mother had read her stories from the time she was two years old. By the time she had enrolled in kindergarten at five, she already knew how to read at the second- or third-grade level. She also had been encouraged to follow a pattern of TV viewing in which alternatives to Walt Disney were historical drama, documentaries, nature programs, and televised classical music, rather than mindless violent cartoons and slasher films.

Emily was a civilized child—too civilized for some of her classmates. Most of the children liked her, and the teacher doted on her, but two or three of the wilder boys seemed to use her for a punching bag. Neither the teacher, a grandmotherly woman nearing a long-awaited retirement, nor the principal, who had some health problems, was able to do much about it. In a way, I sympathized with them. Laws that affect a teacher's right to discipline are so limiting that a teacher has few alternatives in the case of a berserk preadolescent except to hope that the offender will be "classified" and sent to waste his or her time in Special Education.

That, however, did not mean anybody else had the right to use Emily as a human punching bag—even if the teachers and principal couldn't do anything about it.

On the other side of the issue is education itself. Her teacher spent so much time disciplining a few wild kids that the majority of the students didn't receive any education worthy of the name. I spoke with the unfortunate and well-meaning woman at some length and discovered that Emily would be spending the first two years of her school career learning things she already knew. She could already read. She could already count. In fact, she wouldn't learn anything new until the third grade. The whole thing was a waste of her time.

Then the cold and flu season hit. In three months Emily caught five different colds and viruses. In one case she ran a fever of 103, and her baby brother, Johnny, caught the same flu and his fever shot up to 103.7. A good friend of ours had lost his oldest son to a sudden high fever, and comparing his case to ours left my wife almost hysterical. We were on the verge of taking Johnny to the hospital emergency room when the fever finally broke. Emily missed a week of school and coughed for another two weeks. There was no mystery about where she was picking up all these colds. Everybody's children came down with them. Our next-door neighbor's daughter was so chronically feverish that she was 10 pounds underweight and spent more time at home sick than in class.

This situation was too high a price to pay for an education already being criticized as one of the worst in the industrial world.

What did I want from the schools? First and foremost, I wanted a real education for my children—rock-solid basics like the alphabet, simple reading, and simple math, begun as early as possible so that the child would develop skills on a level with her intelligence. The bright child, or any child that isn't academically disabled, can learn to work at a level years ahead of the ordinary public-school class with no trouble at all and very little pressure, if he or she isn't held back by classmates who can't or won't study.

I also wanted an educational program that included Christianity and the Bible as a regular part of the curriculum. I'm a believing Christian myself, and I think Christianity has been the single greatest constructive influence in my life. I don't want that influence denied to my children, especially in an era when some segments of the entertainment industry promote rampant promiscuity, drugs, violence, bigotry, and Satanism in the same way commercials are used to sell soap or stockings. Children today can't afford to be without a firm background of religious faith and morality. I realize that the public schools can't get involved in promoting sectarian religious programs for legal reasons. Thus the schools themselves can't be blamed for this negative aspect of education. But the parents can, and will, be blamed if they fail to provide children with a living faith supported both by teaching and day-to-day living.

Basic studies, Christianity, and then—culture. I wanted my children to be exposed to the full range of world cultures, with particular emphasis on the Bible, Greece, Rome, the

Middle Ages, Great Britain, and the United States. The colleges are trying to bring this emphasis back, but the right place to start is in the lowest grades of elementary school, when values are still being formed and learning patterns established.

I had read about Marva Collins, a black teacher from Chicago who had started her own school, taking in children that the public schools didn't want or couldn't handle. Using her own strong Christian faith and a curriculum based on the Bible and literary classics from Aesop through Shakespeare, she created a school where underachievers and nonachievers turned into overachievers and superachievers. The Bible and the classics had been the keys, along with Mrs. Collins' remarkable devotion to her students and to sane traditional values. My children weren't black, and the neighborhood wasn't a slum, but I had to wonder if her methods might not work better than whatever was occuring in the public schools where Emily was often beaten up by white kids from middle-class families.

There was one other special concern: foreign languages. Emily wanted to be an opera singer; I wanted her to appreciate world cultures. The key to achieving these goals was mastering one or more foreign languages. And the only time this learning can be done with an average student is between the ages of 5 and 10. That's how the Germans, the Dutch, and the Japanese teach their children English, starting in the second or third grades, while few Americans take a foreign language before senior high school. By that time, sports, dating, cars, and the need for easy A's on report cards have swallowed up most of the enthusiasm that might have made learning a foreign language fun—and comparatively easy.

No public school in my area—certainly not the one that demanded two thirds of my property taxes every year—could provide this kind of education. Christianity is officially banned. A few years ago, an otherwise adequate teacher was fired after giving out some very mild religious pamphlets to students who had asked to see them. I didn't like this mentality, especially since the schools were available conduits to distribute all sorts of information I didn't agree with. But like most Americans, I supposed I had to learn to live with it. Foreign languages couldn't be offered because many students or parents were not interested, and because few if any teachers in elementary schools, were capable of teaching them.

As for the basics of reading, math, history, and science, the prevailing philosophy my wife and I encountered was that it was more important for the students to "feel good about themselves" than to actually learn or know anything.

Examine this philosophy in the light of international statistics. American kids routinely score lower in math than the students of any other industrial nation, including not only England, France, Germany, the Soviet Union, and Japan, but also places like South Korea and the Republic of Ireland. You have to go deep into the Third World before you find worse mathematicians than young Americans. Meanwhile, our English scores are the lowest in the English-speaking world. We may not be able to do math as well as the Japanese, but we still speak better English than they do—so far.

Across the board, however, 22 to 25 million native-born Americans are functional illiterates. This condition is true not only in the rural south, but in middle-class school districts. Millions of other Americans—perhaps a near-majority among younger people—are voluntary illiterates. They *can* read, but don't. The inability of employers to find literate employees has led many large corporations to start their own educational programs—a tacit announcement that, in all too many cases, the public schools have failed America, and failed the children and families they were founded to educate and serve.

We put all this information together and came up with an answer that worked for us. My wife and I agreed to educate Emily at home for at least one or two years and see how it worked. Against the advice of almost everyone, ranging from the public school officials to my own parents and many of our friends, we took what many people considered an insane step and did it ourselves.

The experiment was a success. We enjoyed home schooling so much that instead of one or two years we taught Emily at home from the middle of kindergarten through the end of the fourth grade. When Emily reentered school at the beginning of the fifth grade, she was viewed with curiosity, rather than hostility, by peers who'd had a chance to rub the rough spots off one another and had grown up a little since they made her life miserable in kindergarten. She was now an object of envy: "You didn't have to go to school? Wow! I wish *I* didn't have to go to school!"

When test time came, Emily scored in the 97–99 percentile range of the California Tests for fifth grade. These formal tests were the first she had ever taken. In her second year, she scored straight 99s in all academic subjects. She earned the right to take the early SAT tests sponsored by Johns Hopkins University. In the winter of her first year in junior high school, she took these tests and was one of the four top-scoring students in the entire early testing program. She also was admitted to the Junior National Honor Society and made straight A's on her report card, while still finding time for the school newspaper, the school chorus, the church choir, and various family projects. She sang and played the piano in public, and one of her drawings was displayed in a county-wide art contest.

The "freak" had become an academic star instead of an antisocial burnout.

Many bright children score well on tests if they commit their entire lives to study. In Emily's case, she had more free time than most of her peers in school. While other kids were bogged down in endless repetitive homework, Emily completed all her superstar-producing lessons in three or four hours a day and had the rest of her time free for voluntary reading, field trips, nature study, church activities, and even, believe it or not, carefully monitored TV-watching for several hours per day.

We formulated a similar program for my son, Johnny. His character and personality was different than Emily's. Emily had an instinctive love for frills and lace. Johnny liked trucks and guns. Emily enjoyed dancing, but she was basically non-athletic. Johnny liked sports and climbed trees, road signs, and unheated steampipes with the speed and dexterity of a monkey. When his sister tried to make him play dress up, he always wanted to wear a uniform, preferably with an attached gun or sword. Emily was a real little lady. Johnny was a Kid Commando.

The problems Johnny would have faced in mainstreaming were perhaps more formidable than Emily's. He probably would have fit into the noisy, rambunctious crowd so well that he would have quickly discarded academics for athletics—if not delinquency. He needed special help for just the opposite reason that Emily did. She hated school and wasn't learning anything. Johnny might have liked school, but he would have learned even less.

Home education worked for us, but it isn't for everybody. My wife was a state-certified secondary school teacher, and I had a state college degree and had written four books, about a hundred magazine articles, and thousands of newspaper stories, besides having 12 credits of psychology and fluency in two foreign languages. If the schools had wanted to challenge our credentials as full-time home educators, they would have been on very thin ice.

More to the point, we were in a special situation. My wife and I had made the decision when we had children that she would be a full-time homemaker until the youngest child was at least five or six years old. That's probably an old-fashioned way to live, but it's about the only way to live that makes full-time home schooling really practical. The fact that Johnny was four years younger than Emily meant that my wife would be home until Emily was at least nine or ten in either case. She had time between housework and part-time, in-house translating and typing jobs to provide Emily with a full-time mother and supervisor and at least a part-time teacher. My own work was largely done at night. I'm a newsman by profession and evening work is fairly typical of my occupation. I was able to be home many mornings and afternoons and contribute about 60 percent of the actual teaching time.

Most people aren't in that situation. The necessity of the two-income family among people who aren't economic superachievers or the heirs of large fortunes is almost universal. In the 1950s, only about 40 percent of women worked outside the home, but the figure for the 1990s is 65 percent and rising. Meanwhile, the number of single-parent families has more than doubled in the past 20 years, from 3.8 million in 1970 to nearly 9.4 million in 1988. A family in which the mother works full time, and more particularly in which the mother is the only breadwinner, isn't set up for home schooling. The potential tragedy is that those parents who are so dedicated to their children that they're working three or four jobs between them are shortchanging the child on the two most precious assets of any child's life—real parents and a real education.

There is a way out. It's called supplemental home education.

I'm committed to home education as the best way to fly for my own family. But I admit that the way my family economics are operating now I don't have the free time I did five years ago. Yet, by teaching Emily and Johnny at home, I discovered something heartening and helpful: the amount of time consumed by actually educating the home-schooled child can be compressed with no great pressure into three or, at most, four hours a day, with some full days over the weekend for field trips and cultural enrichment. That's all it took. And it produced two happy, unpressured academic superachievers praised by everyone, including their teachers, once they were back in school, as two of the brightest and nicest children they've ever met.

Most parents today can't possibly afford the time it takes for a full-fledged home school operation, with one parent on deck full-time and the other available for regular contributions of teaching and transportation. But most families can find an hour, even two hours a day in their schedule—and that's all it will take to offer the core of this program, particularly if the public schools the child attends fill in some of the basics and most of the frills.

The schools, ironically, tend to fall short on the basics and to handle some of the extras rather well. They have trouble teaching children to read and love reading, to write clearly, and to understand the fundamentals of math. They are usually quite good at offering elective courses in art and music, at least in the suburbs. You can work hand-in-hand with most of the better school systems to ensure that your child gets a first-class ticket in education—and the schools will sometimes thank you for doing it.

Once my children were enrolled back in school, the teachers regularly invited me to lecture to my children's classes on newspapers, creative writing, American Indians, and the artifacts of biblical and classical history. They weren't hostile to home schooling at all; they were favorably impressed at the dedication my wife and I had shown, and the results we had produced.

The information in this book is geared to either the full-time home schooler or, more particularly, the mother or father who wants to know how to teach the basics to and provide the enrichments for the child who is a bright or adequate learner and is getting shortchanged by the school system. There's enough here to provide an enriched education for a future honor student up to the fifth or sixth grade, though the assumed curriculum is three or four years after kindergarten. The parent who wishes to teach full time at home, using this book and the resources it recommends, will be able to do so more easily than he or she thinks. Contrary to the endemic fear of truant officers and being hauled into court, home schooling is legal in all 50 states. The parent who wishes to home school needs only to prove that his or her child is involved in some sort of regular study program and maintaining an academic progress roughly equal to the average child in public schools. Assuming that the home schooled student has a normal IQ and the parent follows the instructions in this book with love, concern, and dedication, meeting those standards should be easy.

This book is also offered to those people who can't find the time to home teach because of job commitments but feel that the schools may be letting their children down. Such parents will find whatever they need in here to assure that their children between the ages of 5 and 10 will learn to read, from the most basic steps with the alphabet and decoding to the thrill of enjoying Bible stories and children's classics from around the world. They'll find a no-fail way to teach basic mathematics so clearly, solidly, and thoroughly that the child will find grade school math a breeze and be encouraged to take—and score well in—the more advanced mathematics courses once they reach high school. They'll find a way to combine reading history with TV viewing in a way that makes the child love reading and appreciate Christian and Western culture, while respecting other cultures and religions in a civilized manner. They'll find ways to give the child a solid grounding in at least one foreign language—my daughter ultimately learned four—even if the parent doesn't speak or read the foreign language in question. They'll find a way to organize "family-only" field trips that can make a museum as exciting as an amusement park. And they'll find methods for evaluating the child's progress, whether the child is in or out of school, in time to correct any problems before they turn into tragedies.

Does it all sound too good to be true? It isn't. If you love your kids as much as my wife and I love ours, you'll find that the hard work involved turns into more fun than you could possibly imagine once you get past a few of the rough spots at the beginning of the voyage.

And just to show you how easy it really is—let's get started right now!

O N E

How to Teach Reading

Five-year-old John Wesley knew what to expect on his birthday. His mother, Susanna Wesley, sat him down and began to teach him the alphabet, just as she had to his older brothers and sisters. By the end of the first lesson, which lasted most of the day, John Wesley, later to be the founder of Methodism, knew all 26 letters of the alphabet and could even read a little poem by sounding out the words.

That story should take the fear out of any home teacher's attitude toward reading. John Wesley mastered the basics in one day with the help of a dedicated and loving mother.

But there's another story that should be considered—the story of John Stuart Mill. Mill was educated by a father who pushed him much too hard. He could read and write classical Greek at the age of 5. By 10, he had mastered more information than what 98 out of 100 college graduates know today. But there was a negative side to this stern force-feeding. Mill suffered a nervous breakdown, lost his faith in God, and was tormented by all sorts of imaginary illnesses. Unable to accept the concept of a loving God because his own father had treated him with such strictness at an early age, Mill struggled to save suffering humanity with all sorts of social schemes—schemes that today are regarded as outmoded.

Like Charles Darwin and Thomas Henry Huxley, he turned an unhappy childhood into a lifelong subconscious war against God. He also suffered, as Darwin and Huxley did, from symptoms of depression. In Darwin's and Huxley's cases, this depression turned them into virtual cripples by the time they were in their middle 30s—still young men in their era or in ours.

These examples are the two lessons of Christian home schooling. Love makes the lesson work. Too much harshness ruins it. The point of Christian home schooling is to produce a splendidly educated adult whose faith in God is intact and whose response to Christian morality is a wholesome acceptance and not a chronic rebellion. Love is a big part of the lesson in Christian home schooling.

You may be surprised to find out just how easy it is to teach a child to read if you don't try to do it all in one day, as Susanna Wesley did. Slow and steady wins the race.

First of all, there's the alphabet.

You've got a valuable ally here. It's called "Sesame Street."

When "Sesame Street" first started on PBS, it was billed as an attempt to give underprivileged children a head start by having TV explain the alphabet and numbers to them, the way a mother or a nanny would explain them to a child of privilege. The lively graphics, the puppets, and the other eye-catching features made "Sesame Street" so popular that it developed into a major entertainment event in most children's lives.

The show's popularity has caused some criticism of "Sesame Street." Some parents think it's too urban—in other words, that it shows too many minorities and not enough middle American types. Others say that the rapid shifts of scenes are so fast that children who grow up watching it regularly may develop trouble with their attention spans. My own feeling is that any objections are null and void when weighed against the single greatest merit of "Sesame Street"—it's a genuine educational show that kids love to watch, and it really does teach the alphabet, numbers, and simple words. It's also the reason that a certain number of children—usually those with caring parents—enter school every year prepared for reading, and sometimes able to read without being taught.

My suggestion is that you either start or finish your preschooler's first instruction with "Sesame Street." If you're reading this book, the chances are that you already have.

But "Sesame Street" won't do the whole job for you. You should also begin the process of reading instruction, even before your child is officially old enough to start school. It's easy. The first step is to sit beside your child and read a story from a picture book at least once, better yet, twice a day. This process should start when the child is two years old— long, long before you begin formal training in the alphabet.

Don't expect the child to start reading yet. What the child learns is to feel that reading is a fun thing to do, and that Mom and Dad, who should alternate in the reader's job, are loving parents.

With this sort of preparation, the actual experience of formal reading instruction should be put off until the child is ready—usually the right age is about four for a girl and five for a boy. (All surveys seem to show that girls mature earlier and are usually a year to 18 months ahead of boys, especially in verbal skills. Some authorities say this distance narrows or even reverses in the late teens. My wife thinks otherwise. She says it lasts forever.)

I learned about this gap between boys and girls the hard way. Johnny taught me. We'd had such good success teaching Emily to read when she was barely four that I started Johnny at the same age. Although he knew the alphabet, he wasn't ready. He just didn't want to string the words together. I was perturbed and pushed him harder. He pushed back. At one point, when I called him for his reading, he shouted at me: "I HATE reading! I HATE U-P-—up!"

My own father would have crammed the note paper down my gullet if I had ever talked to him like that. But I think I know a little more about psychology than he did. The idea was to get Johnny to love reading—not to prove that I was tougher than a four-year-old. I've never much cared for bullies. I decided to back off for six months and let Johnny mature a little bit. So I dropped the formal attempts to get him to decode and concentrated, with my wife's help, on just reading stories to him.

Six or seven months down the road, when he was still short of five, I tried him out on "U-P-—up" again and he took right up on it. Within a few lessons, he was relaying the letters into words like nobody's business.

"The fat cat sat on the hat . . . So what's the big deal?"

Hard-liners, whose eyes glitter and nostrils flare at the word *discipline* and who can't say "love" without blushing, may think I made a big mistake by accepting Johnny's word that he wasn't ready to read at four. I don't think so. He knew, better than I did, what his capacity was.

When the child knows the alphabet forward and back, and when he or she is ready, the actual teaching begins. You just get some sheets of paper and write out the simple one-syllable words, so the child can see you do it, and voice the letters and words as you do it. Kids this age are fantastic mimics. They will be able to follow what you're doing and recognize the words when they see them—provided you show them the same list of words each day, until they know them perfectly.

There's a temptation here to turn up the heat too fast, to use a new set of words each time the child knows *most* of the words on the list. Avoid it. The child needs a stable footing. You should keep repeating the lists of words, with plenty of praise and enthusiasm, until the child knows them all perfectly, and then repeat them and praise some more. A child needs to hear 10 words of praise for every negative word you utter.

Reading is serious. That doesn't mean it can't be fun to learn. The distinction between *serious* and *fun* is probably maintained in the schools because children having fun in groups tend to go wild and get out of control. Your own child, being in a one-on-one situation, is easier to control. So why not have some fun while studying the basics?

Remember Alphabet Soup? Make it a regular part of the menu while you're teaching the alphabet and basic reading. Let the child "play with the food," just this once, to pick out letters or spell out words.

You can also make "alphabet cookies" or "alphabet rolls." Buy or make some dough, cut or roll it into strips, and shape the strips of dough into letters of the alphabet. The child can help shape the dough letters, watch them bake, and help eat them—only after naming each letter.

There are also alphabet blocks. Children enjoy spelling out simple words with these materials, and it's a break from the routine of doing the same thing on paper. But be careful that you buy blocks only of nontoxic plastic or hardwood. Some children, even at this age, will gnaw on the blocks and get paint or wood chips in their mouths. Also be careful about picking up the blocks after playtime. If you've ever been rushing to keep an appointment and stepped on a wooden alphabet block with your instep, then you've experienced one of the most painful moments in home schooling.

Paper is safer, and that's what you'll need next—a lot of paper. You can stock up in bulk, or you can do what we did and use scrap paper most of the time.

Sit the child down by your side, or on your lap, and write _____OT.

Write it a few times, in a column, like this:

_____OT
_____OT
_____OT
_____OT

Now ask the child to put letters of the alphabet in the blank space. See if they make words.

Pronounce each sound the child makes, and ask the child to pronounce it with you. Then pick out which sounds are words. *Dot* and *pot* and *lot* are words, but some of the others won't be.

Change one letter of the semiword. Make it _____AT.

_____AT
_____AT
_____AT
_____AT

Now the child will really have fun. You can make a lot of simple words by adding first letters to _____AT.

This procedure may seem simple to you, but remember, it's probably the first time the child has seen it. Don't think he or she is slow if it takes a while to sink in. And don't ever become verbally abusive if the child has trouble with it. Release your frustrations by hugging and cheering every time the child gets one right.

You can work your way through a lot of combinations by using a vowel and a final T to make short words. The same is true of a vowel and a final N.

If you're good at drawing pictures — or even if you aren't — you may want to draw pictures of the words the child is spelling.

Next you can try the words that end with single or double vowels. The semiword _____EE has lots of possiblities.

By now you'll probably understand that you can save yourself some time if you make copies of a few dozen semiword pages. If you have the time, it may be just as well to write out all the _____OT and _____AT and _____IT and _____EE words in neat columns and let the child fill them in. But if you're pressed for time, some copies of these lessons will help save hours over the course of the first months of reading instruction. You'll want to spend anywhere from 10 to 30 minutes a day letting the child fill in these columns of semiwords. These steps are the first toward reading (and spelling), and just as in learning to walk, the first steps are usually slow and faltering. But, just as your child takes off quickly once he or she actually learns to toddle, your child will begin reading actual small words and simple sentences almost before you know it.

I recommend the process of writing each letter as the child

learns to spell the word for two reasons. The first is that children have a natural need for attention from their parents. If they learn to associate this attention with reading they'll learn to love reading. The second is that the child will remember the letter better if he sees how it's made. This activity may later help him learn to write.

The alternatives to this old fashioned reliance on pen or pencil and paper, other than "Sesame Street," are not what I would recommend. You can buy computer programs (or borrow them from libraries), which will help the child learn the letters and words. Some of these materials may be fine, but many computers, especially the older models with the coarser screen images, could be irritating to young and growing eyes. Contrary to the myths circulated by computer sales people, children don't instantly become smarter by staring at a computer screen, or by playing computerized versions of the games you and I once played with paper and pencils. Some short exposure to computer word learning probably won't hurt. I would never rely on computers, however, to teach reading. Mothers and fathers do it far better. And that's a big part of home teaching.

There are more traditional aids I recommend. At most book stores and even some paper and pharmacy stores you can buy books that teach basic reading. The Golden *Step Ahead* books and the older Golden *Fun at Home* Workbooks are good supplements to your own handwritten lesson papers, with color illustrations children like.

Many books are available to help parents teach reading, either as an alternative or a supplement to school. You can buy as many or as few of these books as you like. I think a few of them can be helpful. The best teaching aids, however, are the same colorful story books you've been using to teach your child a love for books.

Once the child is *decoding* simple words, let your child go over some of his or her old favorite stories with you. This time move your finger along the page and voice each word you come to, and let the child repeat. The next time, move your finger along and let the child say the word, if he or she can. Don't make a big deal out of trying to prove how little he or she knows. If the child doesn't learn it in a few seconds, explain without rebuke what the word is. But if you continue in the same book day after day, the child *will* get it either by learning to read or by memorizing the story. And the child will soon find that reading is easier than memorizing.

You can pick your own books for this activity. Emily liked *Scuffy the Tugboat,* and some of the other Little Golden Books. Johnny's favorite was the "Johnny Lion" series— probably because of the similar names. Having a book they like, and a teacher who loves them, are the two greatest assets any child can enjoy while learning to read. All it takes on your part is a certain amount of patience. I got a little tired of Johnny Lion until Johnny Koster started to read the words from cover to cover without any coaching. Now I remember Johnny Lion with affection—and gratitude.

Johnny Lion got to be such a favorite, both with me and with my wife, that when she saw a plush puppet that looked just like Johnny Lion, she bought it on the spot. We mounted the plush lion over the couch corner where we took turns teaching Johnny to read. Sometimes when Johnny Koster had a particularly tough time with new words, we would take Johnny Lion off the wall and use him to read along with Johnny. This exercise sounds sillier than it is. When the child is exploring reading for the first few months, anything that makes the exercises enjoyable rather than threatening is worth doing.

We had used a similar mascot with Emily when she was younger. Sometimes I couldn't be at home when she did the lessons I usually taught. So to console her, I would leave her lessons clasped in the arms of "Mrs. Brown" for Emily to find when she got up. "Mrs. Brown" was a sort of brown plush spaniel, which clasped a baby spaniel in a Velcro grip. The space between "Mrs. Brown's" arms could hold not only the baby dog, but a rolled-up lesson in reading or math, plus a note once Emily had learned to read. Somehow it seemed a more personal way to leave a message than to stick it on the refrigerator.

Little gestures like this one are important. So is patience. We all tend to take reading for granted. The 22 million Americans who can't read properly, and the millions of others who never read when they can avoid it, know otherwise. That's why you have to make sure you sit down with the child every day for at least a half hour of study.

Some hard-core educators insist that children should learn every word phonetically—by the sound of letters—and not rely in any way on visual scanning to recognize the word. I don't see how their system is even possible, let alone desirable. As you read this passage, how many of the words do you stop to sound out, a letter at a time? Probably none of them. The secret of fluent reading isn't sounding out each word, though it's important to know how to do it, in a pinch. The secret is reading actively, and avidly, to build first understanding, then speed, and finally a large vocabulary. That's the method I used with both of my kids. I don't know if it's old-fashioned or newfangled, progressive or reactionary. I *do* know that Emily scored 98s and 99s in all aspects of reading when she took her California Tests after returning to school. When she took her first swat at the SATs—in seventh grade at the age of 12—she scored a 550 in verbal.

The schools turn reading into a big deal because the schools have failed to teach reading to a shocking percentage of students. If you start a child off at the right age, however, they can go from the first glimpse of the alphabet to free reading of simple books, not in one day, but in a matter of a few months. The missing ingredient is a parent or parents who care. After you have started them off reading—and I recommend you do it before they start the school's reading program—it's still pleasant to sit beside them for reading time every day. But now *they* can read *you* the story.

T W O

How to Teach Math

Just how badly even good schools do at teaching basic mathematics was brought home to me by Daisaku.

Daisaku wasn't one of the Japanese educators who invent things like violin for toddlers or super-math for everybody. He was a skinny teenager who showed up one chilly January day and asked if I wanted my snow shoveled.

At this point in my life, I was working 60 hours a week and was glad to be able to find somebody to take snow-shoveling off my hands. I had tried other kids around the neighborhood, both white and black. None of them had proved reliable. Daisaku had a rudimentary command of English and had trouble keeping himself from bowing when he talked. But he looked reliable. So I gave him a tryout.

Daisaku showed up without fail the first couple of times it snowed. One time I looked out and saw a girl a few years younger than Daisaku shoveling the snow. My wife went out and held a conversation with the girl in Japanese.

"It's Daisaku's sister," my wife explained. "He's studying for a big test so he sent her to make sure the snow got shoveled."

The system worked so well that Daisaku and the sister were recalled during the summer, when I had to be out of town, to help my wife with various gardening projects. They got to be regular fixtures. There were three younger sisters—Daisaku was the only boy in the family—and the little kids drafted Emily into their play group.

Daisaku liked me. I know because, according to my wife, he called me by a nickname that means "Uncle Bear." This term is a great compliment among the Japanese—or so she said.

One day, Daisaku, looking mortified, came up to my wife and told her: "Tell Uncle Bear I can't shovel your snow any more this year—I will send my sister."

I talked this over with my wife, Shizuko, while Daisaku made discreet faces at Johnny, who was then a toddler and riding on her back. Daisaku liked Johnny because Johnny couldn't "speak," as he put it, and didn't have any trouble understanding Daisaku's English.

"What's the problem with Daisaku?" I asked. She interrogated him while Johnny watched in dread fascination as the strange language poured out of their mouths.

"He says he has a full-time job at a gas station," my wife said.

"Great!" I said. "All the American kids are out of work, and they give the job to Nephew Bear here. Does he have a driver's license?"

After some more interrogation, even my wife had an expression of disbelief on her face. Daisaku kept assuring her he was telling the truth.

"He says that Tom and Andy both had the job, but they couldn't do it because they couldn't make change," she said. "It was Andy who gave it to him. He introduced Daisaku to the station manager and told him that he was the only guy in the group who could make change."

"American no make change," Daisaku said.

So the next winter, Daisaku's sister showed up whenever it snowed while Daisaku pumped gas because none of his American friends—college-bound high school seniors—could do enough mental math to make change when the bill said

$10 and the gas meter said $8.50.

I hope I'm wrong, but this example may be American history in a condensed and localized version. When the labor pool of Americans consists of 18-year-old kids who don't know how to change a 20-dollar bill, gas station managers will hire a Japanese who speaks poor English rather than go out of business or pay $25 an hour for a college math major.

And that's why we should start taking math very seriously. The international economic scene and the service station business have much the same attitude toward people who can't do math.

The three keys to teaching math at home are: start early, practice often, and keep it interesting. And in math, even more than in most subjects, the absolute bottom line is that you can't neglect the basics. If you do, you'll trip over them before you have a chance to get much beyond them.

The first thing you have to teach, obviously, is the numbers from 1 to 10. Here, as in reading, "Sesame Street" is an ally not to be overlooked. Turn it on and make sure the child watches it, each and every day, as soon as the child's neck sets. If the child hasn't learned the numbers from 1 to 10, by sight and name, by the time the child is five, you may have serious problems.

Personal interaction should reinforce all TV instruction. Children should not be raised by TV alone—though all too many are. Count your own fingers, then let the child count his or hers. The hands (and feet) were the first calculators. That's why the number 20 is called a *score*—people used to keep score on their fingers and toes.

The next step is to buy an old-fashioned but effective piece of teaching equipment: a counting frame. This simple wooden frame has colored beads strung up on steel wires—10 beads to each wire, for a total of 50. You can find one at any store that stocks education toys. I got mine at a general discount store that stocked everything from greeting cards to lawn furniture. If you or someone you know is handy, you can make one.

The uses of the counting frame are many. First, the child should learn to count from 1 to 50 by ticking off the beads, one at a time. You should make a big and favorable fuss each time the child rounds out a set of 10. Learning to think in tens is important. The best time to start the counting is around the age of four.

Once the child has the counting mastered, it's time to master groups of numbers. Tick off a random number of beads and ask how many of them there are. The child is allowed to touch them while counting. Praise the child when he or she answers correctly. Remember that while it may take a long time to master such a simple skill when the child is only four or five, it will be retained better and allow for faster future progress when it's learned early. But walk a fine line between encouraging the child and browbeating him or her into disliking the lessons—and the teacher.

Some children will have such a natural affinity for math that they will actually enjoy these simple lessons, especially if they're praised and rewarded. Other children may be less fascinated. Persist. Basic math is a necessity of life. My daughter, Emily, showed an amazing resistance to math almost from her first lesson. I later learned that her dislike was because somebody close to her had told her that "girls aren't good at math." This adult advice is the kind that no child needs. I convinced her that *one*—this isn't true; and *two*—I wasn't accepting any excuses like that for not finishing her lesson every day. By the time she was back in public school, she was routinely scoring 98s and 100s in math tests, and she scored 98s and 99s in the California Test. Overcoming the prejudice that "girls aren't good at math" was the single most important aspect of her success. My son, on the other hand, must have been told that "boys are good at math," because he always seemed to have an affinity for arithmetic. His prejudice was worth retaining. Hers had to be discarded.

It was at the next step that I had to battle Emily's prejudice against her own math ability.

This exercise is useful in teaching *place value*. When you

tell the child that numbers acquire value by their place, the child probably won't understand. You then tell the child that all numbers in the right-hand column are one-digit numbers. The child probably won't undertand that statement either. So you draw a dot on the paper. This dot is a decimal point. You now tell the child that the number on the left side of this decimal point has a value of one. Now the child may begin to understand what you're talking about. But don't panic if the child still doesn't. Every psychological study I've ever read or heard about shows that children below the age of 9 or 10, no matter how quickly they learn, have little or no capacity to handle abstract ideas. (The two or three children out of a thousand who *do* handle abstraction well at this age are puzzling to the researchers, though they're a joy to their parents.)

So you work backward to teach this vital abstraction. Get a magazine or a newspaper. Set the counting frame up on a stable table. Then let the child find a "big" number in the magazine or newspaper—one with four or five digits.

"All right," you say. "Now you'll learn how to express that number on the counting frame."

Say that the number the child picks is 1,244. You tell the child this:

The bottom row of the counting frame will stand for the ones. Tick off four *ones*. The child does this, counting out loud. "Now let the second line of beads from the bottom stand for *tens*. Tick off four *tens*. The child may appear confused at first, but if your instructions are clear, the hands-on part of the drill should go perfectly. "Now let the third line of the counting frame stand for *hundreds*. Tick off two *hundreds*.

"Now listen up and listen tight. This is it. The big one. The fourth line of the counting frame stands for *thousands*. Pick out one *thousand* and tick it off."

When the child does this activity correctly, make a big fuss over how well the exercise went. Then repeat it four or five more times. The child has now begun to learn abstraction in a way that is concrete and visible.

While the child is mastering abstraction, don't of course, discontinue either "Sesame Street" or the process of counting on fingers and toes. Learning what a number *is* may take a surprising amount of time, but children of bright or adequate intelligence usually have trouble in math only because they haven't understood the basics. They may never have the kind of enthusiasm it takes to make a great world-class mathematician—a love of math that's almost mystical—but if they learn the basics without learning to hate the whole subject, they will avoid any real problems. And even basic math, as we will see, can be a lot of fun.

Practical math is a good way to teach academic math. Let the child help out around the house. Gather up socks or shoes and ask "How many are there?" There's a character on "Sesame Street," obviously inspired by Count Dracula as played by Bela Lugosi, who loves to *count* all kinds of objects. Personally I think most children overdo horror movies. But if "The Count" inspires your child to go around counting birds on a branch, or cars parked on the street, or peas in a pod, it's all to the good.

If you've started the child on "Sesame Street" around the age of three, and started actually counting and using the counting frame by four or four-and-a-half, the child at home should be ready for actual arithmetic by the age of five. In this field, at least, most boys and girls are about equal because, cultural prejudices aside, boys do have an affinity for math just as girls do for reading. These tendencies *never* mean "girls aren't good at math," or that you should accept a mediocre math performance from a bright child because it's cute or feminine to be scatterbrained where numbers are concerned. It just means that boys learn math more easily than girls, resist it less, and like it better. It's a break for the hardworking home teacher that you need less *push* to get boys into math, just as you need less *push* to get girls into reading.

The first lessons are easy. Addition is the subject.

Take the counting frame and sit beside the child. Move one

bead away from the others. Ask how many beads you moved.
"One!"
"That's good! One!"
Now move one more bead so that the first bead and the new bead are side by side, actually touching one another.
"Now how many beads?"
"Two!"
"Very good! One and one are two!"
Now you move over a third bead and repeat. The child will absorb the idea of adding very quickly.

Once you can see the child is completely in control of understanding how "addition" works by simple counting, you move on to groups. Instead of ticking off the beads one by one, you tick off two or three and then add one or two more. I think you will be amazed at how fast a five-year-old picks up the basic concept.

The next thing to remember is to build confidence and proficiency. These only come through practice. The child may not be as bored as you are, so try not to show your boredom. The real fun of math comes later.

Take out a piece of paper and write down all the simple addition problems: $1 + 1 =$ ____, $1 + 2 =$ ____, and so on. When you finish, you should have a whole piece of paper covered with simple one-digit math problems. Try to include all of them.

Now go to the copy shop or the library and bang off about 20 copies on the copier. Save the master sheet for more copies. You may need them.

Once the child has mastered simple addition by the counting frame—this process should take a few weeks to a month—the assignment changes. Each day, as part of the math lesson, the child has one of these sheets to fill out.

Encourage the child in every way you can—short of letting him or her off completely—to find this enjoyable. They can keep the counting frame if they find it comforting. But they must do this lesson *every day* five, or better yet, six days a week. (It's a healthy idea in psychological as well as biblical terms to give the child one day in seven off from formal lessons. I see no reason why home schoolers shouldn't study on Saturdays, however, when they aren't on field trips. The Japanese and some Europeans go to school six days a week and most college kids spend Saturdays studying if they don't have part-time jobs.)

It's at this point that you might want to brighten up your child's lessons with some of the home schooling or enrichment books you can find in book and stationery stores. These materials are usually listed by grade level or, more reliably, by subject. The *Addition and Subtraction* book in one of these series would be a good buy about now. There's nothing in it you can't cover with scrap paper and some copies from the copy shop. But the color cartoon illustrations can brighten up a black-and-white subject.

Addition should also be carried over into everyday life. When you're working in the yard or the kitchen, ask the child: "How many birds are on that branch?" or, "How many apples are in the the bag?" Then, make time to play a game with the apples.

"Here are three apples. Now I'm adding two. How many are there?"

You should try to do this activity once or twice a day, or even more often, if you're not forcing it. The child can experience mathematics as part of everyday life. Not only does this activity make it easier for him or her to learn, it convinces the child that it's important.

Most children will master the basic single-digit addition problems by instant replay in a month or two of daily practice, if you explain it on the counting frame and drill the child six days a week. The actual time consumed, unless the child deliberately decides to dawdle, should be 15 minutes. If the child does decide to dawdle, filling out the form may take three hours. At this point it becomes a contest of wills. My position is this: I've never struck a child for refusal to study or resistance to learning. I hate bullies and don't want to become one. On the other hand, I feel absolutely justified in denying the child the right to leave the house, play with toys, or — most especially — to watch TV until all the math lesson is done — every day. When you think of the harm you will do the child by letting him or her grow up to be a "math idiot," it's worth a few glares and a little whining.

If math resistance doesn't develop into a full-time battle of wills, the child should be ready to start subtraction two months after starting addition. Subtraction is harder than addition because children have trouble with abstract reasoning. Once you get past that barrier, it's just addition in reverse. And that's how you offer it. Show the child the counting frame with all the beads on one side. Have the child count the beads on one line. Unless some are broken, there should be 10 of them.

Now take one away. Ask the child how many beads are left. The child will have to count the beads to know there are nine survivors. Now take one more away. This time the answer may come easier. In any case, go over it a few days on the counting frame before you introduce paper problems. It's hard to understand, but younger children really do encounter some hardship with subtraction.

Now it's time for the paperwork. Write down all the basic one-digit subtraction problems: $2 - 1 = $ ____ ; $3 - 1 = $ ____. You should fill a page with them, and basically strip all the numbers from nine to two down one number at a time by subtracting one, two, three, four, five, six, seven and eight from all the numbers that are larger. *Don't* get involved in negative numbers or zero yet. That area is for a later lesson, farther down the road. One of the worst mistakes the public schools make, however, is starting math basics too late, usually because the constant need for discipline and diversion makes it impossible to start it early. Another serious mistake, made by school teachers and home teachers alike, is to push the brighter or faster students ahead before they have completely mastered the simplest arithmetic. Again, slow and steady wins the race. And if your child starts math at the age of five, he or she has a one- to two-year head start.

The same steps should be used in teaching subtraction. Let the child use the good old counting frame until he or she has the problems memorized. Use kitchen or outdoor games to reinforce the art of subtraction. Use the home schooling books sold in stores as you want to. A few of them can be quite helpful, but it's cheaper, and probably more effective, to make your own lessons with a pen, paper, and a copier.

Your next set of lessons to be mass-copied should feature a mixture of addition and subtraction, about half a page of each. The key here is to make up two or three different sets and stagger them, so that the child isn't doing the same lesson every day. He or she should learn to do the math based on the numbers — not just to recall the answer based on page position. In other words, if the child can remember that he or she gets all the answers correct by writing a series of numbers in the answer-spaces of the first line, the child may contrive to fill out the paper purely from memory, without interacting with the numbers, which is something to avoid at all costs. To make sure it doesn't happen, you can wile away spare moments by scribbling math lessons on scrap paper, backs of envelopes, or junk mail, or whatever else you come across. Parents may want to write lessons at the office during coffee breaks if they aren't directly involved in home teaching. The child has to learn to deal with the problem and solve it, rather than taking "short cuts" that are really "short circuits."

Not counting "Sesame Street" and informal counting exercises, you should by now have been teaching math for about six months. The child should be able to add and subtract one-digit numbers instantly, flawlessly, without using fingers and toes or even the good old counting frame. He or she should be wired for addition and subtraction. If this isn't the case, double up on the lessons for the next few weeks, because you won't want to tackle the Bear until you have all your ducks in a row with addition and subtraction.

The Bear is the times tables.

Let's face it. Learning the times tables isn't easy. It never was. Back in the days of Isaac Newton, Blaise Pascal, and Wilhelm von Leibnitz — the years when modern mathematics emerged with the discovery of calculus and probability — nobody who wasn't a professional mathematician bothered to memorize the times tables. They wrote the answers down and carried them around on crib sheets. Those days are gone forever. The math class of problem students consists almost entirely of tragic youngsters who couldn't do the most basic math because they have never learned the times tables. They never learned because nobody ever forced them to learn. You don't learn the times tables by having an apple hit you on the head. It takes work. But without the times tables, no mathematics exists beyond advanced finger counting.

First step. Get out the old counting frame. The child will learn much faster if he or she understands what he or she is learning.

Take the first row of beads. Tick the beads off into sets of twos. Now do the same to the second line. You should now have ten sets of beads, two beads in each set.

Ask the child how many beads are in one set. That's so easy the child may laugh. Then ask how many there are in two sets.

This activity introduces the concept of sets. It also shows the need for the times tables. You can dramatize this need by playing a game. Ask the child how many beads are in six sets of 2. Then tell the child it's 12 while he or she is still counting. If the child has any curiosity or competitive spirit, he or she will want to know how you did this "magic." Just tell the child you know the times tables. When he or she knows the times tables, the child will be able to do the magic too. For the rest of the first lesson, you may want to divide the counting frame into sets of three beads each and four beads each to play this magic game again. Each child will react differently. Emily, on the one hand, was not instinctively mathematical and needed a lot of encouragement. She was curious but a bit nonchalant about it. Johnny, on the other hand, was so furious because I could bang off these answers instantly and always get them right, that he would paw the ground and flare his nostrils like a bull by the end of the magic game, ready to gore the times tables to death so he could take on Daddy on his own turf.

The first thing to remember is that the times tables is a *lot* of memorizing for a five- or six-year-old. One of the first steps is to combine the times tables with other math lessons. Continue with addition and subtraction. A half-page per day of each is about right, coupled with snap problems that come up in everyday life. "I see three blue cars and two grey ones. How many are there?"

On the bottom of the sheet, before the lesson is considered complete, the child has to write out that day's times tables. You start with the one times table, just to build self-confidence: One times one is one; one times two is two; and so on. The one times table can be mastered in a day.

The two times table actually involves thinking. I suggest you give the child a week of writing this set out every day, and reciting it verbally morning and afternoon. Then try the child out on it—first in order, and then mixed, so he or she can't just prate it out in sing-song fashion. The child *must* know it perfectly before he or she moves on. It should take about two weeks, but even if it takes longer, don't advance beyond the two-times table before the child knows it backward, forward, and upside down.

Tackle each times table one at a time. You'll want to have the child write it out at the end of each lesson that contains addition and subtraction, six days a week.

From now on, your math lessons will need two sheets of paper: the sheet with the copied addition and subtraction problems, and a blank sheet for the times tables. I don't suggest leaving blanks for the child to fill in. The child will remember better if he or she writes out the numbers for the whole problem every day.

You may also want to introduce the store-bought books on multiplication and division at this time. They're a good device for maintaining interest. But they're no substitute for daily drill. Accept no excuses for not writing out the times tables six times a week as far as the child has studied, and for not drilling verbally at least twice a day. It's better too if both parents take turns drilling the child aloud. This shared responsibility helps to prevent the tension that arises in the family when one parent becomes "the softie" and the other becomes "the ogre." Yes, yes. Times tables are tough to remember. But they're absolutely vital.

The optimistic view is that, with regular drill, the child will be able to learn a times table per week. More realistically, a times table every two or three weeks is what you can expect. Once again—it can't be stated too often—even the brightest children don't handle abstractions well. Don't let it infuriate you. It's not the child's fault. And it's not your fault if you sometimes get bored or frustrated going over the times tables. But it *is* your fault if you sluff off and don't make the child learn them, thoroughly and flawlessly. There's no place left in the world for little princes and princesses who get a gentleman's or lady's "C" in basic math and swagger off to gym or flutter off to art. They've got to learn times tables— perfectly.

In my case, I never did. I have vague memories that we had to cram the whole second half of the times tables down in about two weeks to pass some kind of schoolwide test. I memorized them quickly, and forgot them shortly. Through a combination of inspired logic and fudging, I was able to evade detection through my academic career—until I hit Algebra II, where I couldn't cover up fast enough, and got blown out of the water. I was a "math cripple." In some ways I still am. My logical capacities are good enough so that I got straight A's in geometry—without ever learning the upper times tables—but the amount of accurate calculation needed in advanced algebra sank me.

I didn't want this situation to happen to my kids. I drilled them in the times tables until they could do them in their sleep. They whined and objected, but they didn't hate me for it. And when they actually started public schools, they found that math was suprisingly easy, and getting 98s and 100s after finishing their tests first in class was fun.

Here are a couple of tricks to take the sting out of memorizing the times tables.

Make up a real times table like the kind that sea captains used to carry in Isaac Newton's day. You simply get a large sheet of paper with graph ruling to start with. If you can't find one, you fold a sheet of paper into regular squares until it's patterned like a checkerboard. The upper left corner remains blank.

Start from the square just below the blank upper left corner. Write the numbers 2, 3, 4, 5, 6, 7, 8, 9, 10, 11, 12, all the way down.

Now start at the second square on the top line. Write the same numbers 2, 3, 4, and so on from left to right across the top line.

You and your child have to cooperate. You draw one finger down and one across to the place where 2 crosses 2. This space is now blank. But you ask the child "What is two times two?" When you get your answer—assuming it's right—fill it in. Working together, you and your child should fill in the entire times table. Use the counting frame if the child has trouble with the calculations. You can explain that in Ye Olden Days sea captains and pirates had to carry these times tables around under their hats because only a few professional mathematicians memorized the times tables. This fact may make the child feel better if he or she is having trouble with it. Encourage the child, and don't ever slack off.

Another key is to link the memorization to something enjoyable. When my late father was still alive, he and my mother used to take Emily on little trips a couple times a week in the spring, summer, and autumn. I encouraged these trips because the love between children and grandparents is an important lesson of life. I made sure, however, that before Emily left the house, she showed my wife a boarding pass— the entire times table written out, from two through nine, with a fair degree of neatness. Emily tried to escape the hard work of doing the times tables, which she didn't like, into reading, which she already loved. The amount of whining a six-year-old can do in the presence of a supportive grandmother and grandfather is beyond mathematical calculation. But I stood my ground under pressure from everybody (except my wife, who in this case agreed with me completely). Emily didn't leave without the boarding pass, no matter how much she whined and how much it inconvenienced my parents' excursion. She had to understand two things: she was the one causing the inconvenience because she had been given adequate time to finish the lesson; and there was no way I was accepting the cliché that "girls aren't good at math" as an excuse. As the result of my forthright nastiness, Emily knew the times tables perfectly by the time she was seven, and never again did she have any trouble with math — a subject that became one of her best once she started school again.

After my father passed away, I took over the job of chauffeuring the kids to Grandma's. This task also became an opportunity for learning. The children and grandmother needed one another, and they obviously loved one another. Grandma's house was always fun, but the trip was a bore. So I used the half hour on the road to teach Johnny the times tables, verbally, by rote. He would start reciting when we left the driveway, and by the time Grandma's house loomed in the distance he had finished the drill three or four times. He also learned his times tables much faster than Emily.

If you have a computer at home or have access to one at the library's children's room, there are computer programs that help children learn the times tables and other math functions in a way that's very effective, but only after you've begun the learning one-on-one, side by side. This is a better program than any yet devised by a computer company.

After they had already learned the times tables and started to enjoy math, Emily and Johnny discovered a game called *Number Munchers.* The "good guys" in this game are moved around a grid square eating multiples of two, three, four, and so forth, while the "bad guys," called *troggles,* try to eat the "good guys." It's not only harmless fun, but it's an excellent way to get the home or supplemental student started in computers, and to help the times tables go down a little more smoothly. The *Number Munchers* program also features exercises in factors, primes, equality, and inequality. Generally I think the lower grades of some schools overdo the computer trip, and the computer salespeople promise virtually anything, so much so that a lot of adults and kids are turned off from the whole topic. But these games, and a few others, are genuinely educational. Few children will voluntarily spend an hour a day "learning the times tables." A surprising number will spend an hour playing *Number Munchers* or *The Market Place,* which teaches business concepts and math skills of estimating.

The good news is that the worst is over. Once the child has learned the times tables, nothing will be able to stop him or her from making good progress in math, assuming a will to learn and study and any aptitude at all. The lessons, carried out daily, should include a page of addition, a page of subtraction, and a page of times-table math problems, staggered so the child can't perform them by memory based on page order. These three pages of math won't take more than 30 to 45 minutes—less than that if the child is motivated to get done—but they represent the progress that most students achieve in three or four years within the walls of a public school. If you've been lucky and persistent, you've done it in a little over a year. The child now has two or three years to build absolute self-confidence and pressure-proof skill in basic math before you move on to division and the more abstract forms of math. I'll describe some of them in subsequent chapters, but for now it's important to let the child catch his or her breath, develop competence, and shift the focus of his or her intellectual energy temporarily to the next step. And you'll be surprised when you discover what this one is.

THREE

Teaching a Foreign Language (Even When You Don't Know One)

The American school system has made itself ludicrous in international competitions in mathematics and science. There's one field, moreover, in which Americans seldom even dare to compete—the study of foreign languages.

While most Swiss, Canadians, and Belgians, and many Dutch and Germans are bilingual or trilingual, most Americans will shrug and say they have enough trouble with English. It's a sad and sour old joke, and nobody's laughing anymore. The failure of Americans to learn foreign languages is a national disgrace.

Other than wiping out this disgrace, there are a number of good reasons for wanting your child to learn one or more foreign languages. For those children being trained for academic competition, it's proverbial that learning any of the other major Western languages can boost the SAT scores in English by 100 points or more. Proficiency in a second foreign language is often said to add another 50 points. Consider the difference between a 500 and a 650, or between a 600 and a 750, in applying to good colleges or seeking scholarships, and you'll see that a foreign language is a superb academic investment.

Second, there is what could crassly be called "snob appeal." I'll remember for the rest of my life the time Johnny, Emily, and I were exploring one of the gift shops at the Metropolitan Museum of Art in quest of a present for my wife. She hadn't been able to come to New York City with us, but we knew just what book she wanted for Christmas — so we ordered it. The manager didn't seem impressed until she heard me pronounce the name of the book: *Les Très Riches Heures de Jean, Duc de Berry.* It was a miserably cold day in December with slush falling on Fifth Avenue, but the fact that I had pronounced the name correctly thawed out the elegant blond lady at the gift shop completely. It was like springtime indoors. Where did my son prep? Did my daughter study ballet? We were instantly welcomed into the fold of the Four Hundred just because the kids and I could say a few words in French with a passable accent. The lady was even more impressed when I told her that my children had *prepped* at home and that my son also spoke some German.

"And you, dear?" the lady asked Emily.

Emily smiled in refined embarrassment and replied, *"Français . . . Deutsch . . . Italiano . . . Español."*

Emily's roster of language skills brings up the first big question: Which language (or languages) do you teach your children?

With Emily, the choices fell into place by themselves. From the time she was a toddler in her playpen, she had been singing along with the music from operas and operettas on the hi-fi or the radio. She didn't understand the words, of course, but her mimicry of the sounds and her ability to follow the melodies were impressive. When I first began to contemplate taking her out of kindergarten, but before I actually made up my mind, I started to teach her both French and German. I knew both languages quite well and they're both important in opera and classical music. At first she objected: "The other kids in kindergarten don't hafta study French and German! Why do *I* hafta study French and German?" This reply naturally prejudiced me against kindergarten almost as much as the punchings, the head colds, and the educational void. When the peer group starts to talk through your kid's mouth, it's time to disabuse her of the peer group, which in later years becomes the conduit for drugs, alcohol, sexual promiscuity, vandalism, reckless driving, and the unquestioned belief that learning is worthless and school is only a fun place to hang out.

Over protests from Emily—and my mother, who took Emily's side—I persisted in teaching her French and German.

My mother's generation was the generation of the "100 percent Americans"—the generation in which both recent immigrants and people who had lived in America for two or three generations were encouraged to break all ties with Europe. In the aftermath of World War I, with most of Europe teetering on the brink of either Communism or fascism, there was some point in constantly telling people they were Americans and had no ties to Europe. This attitude, however, was the beginning of cultural illiteracy. The American public schools German-language program sank when the U-20 torpedoed the *Lusitania* in 1915. Before that, German had been 3 times more popular in American schools than French, and 30 times more popular than Spanish. During World War I, the Germans became "The Huns," and the state of Nebraska made it a crime for a father to teach his son German in the privacy of his own home. Later, German was associated with the Nazis and Italian with Mussolini's fascists. Both languages—important to culture and the arts, to international business, to the cosmopolitan appreciation of life—died on the vine. French survived among people who were dedicated to a strenuous academic program or to an international lifestyle, but even French is far less popular in school curriculums than it was 20 or 30 years ago, simply because foreign languages, started after the age of 10 or 12, are really quite difficult.

People of my parents' generation, except for the very rich and the very educated, became obsessively monolingual by rote. All through school they were hammered with a simplistic message: Americans speak English . . . Americans speak English . . . Americans speak English.

The irony is that any American who is fluent in a major European language has a staggering advantage both in academics and employment. Check out the classified employment ads in a large urban newspaper and compare the pay rates for any job advertised as bilingual and the same job when there is no need for French or German.

Monolingualism certainly wasn't imposed on Emily. After about a year of studying French and German, she actually enjoyed the lessons. After 18 months, she achieved self-confidence, not only in her knowledge of French and German, but in her ability to learn other languages.

Around this time, we watched Franco Zeffirelli's "The Life of Verdi" on PBS. Emily, previously a partisan of French and German opera, discovered the vivid and colorful world of Italian opera through this film and was transported.

"Dad?" she asked me one day. "Do you suppose I could study Italian too?"

"Are you sure Italian won't make you forget French and German?" I asked.

"No, never," she said. "I love French and German. But there are a lot of good operas in Italian I want to learn."

"OK, Emily," I said. "We'll study Italian."

A few weeks later, Emily had another suggestion.

"You know . . . there's a lot of Spanish stuff around. It's easier to get stuff to study in Spanish than in Italian."

"You mean you want to give up Italian and study Spanish?" I asked dubiously.

"No. I want to study Spanish *and* Italian."

"And French and German?"

"Sure," she said. "There's no way I'd ever forget French and German. They're like my two second languages."

"Are you sure you won't get the Spanish mixed up with the Italian—that you'll be able to tell them apart?"

"*Si, Papa . . . sta bene!*" (Yes, Daddy . . . It's all right!)

We ended up studying French, German, Italian, and Spanish. A year to 18 months after starting each language, she was reading each language at her own grade-level.

Emily today doesn't have any trace of a foreign accent, unless you're from the South, in which case she's readily recognizable as a Yankee. The amazing thing to me is that she speaks all four foreign languages without any recognizable foreign accent. When she reads her school reports about various scientists, pronouncing each name with a perfect native inflection, her teachers look at one another in amazement. Recently, the choir at the church we attend wanted to sing "Silent Night" in German. Nobody, including the pastor and the assistant pastor, who had German surnames, could figure out how to pronounce the words. Somebody found Emily baby-sitting with the toddlers. She soon straightened them right out—adults included.

How was all this possible? There are a number of easy steps, that once followed, make it all possible—even if you don't know the language you're trying to teach.

Pick the language you want to study. The easiest way is to let the child select the language. Picking a foreign language you know, if you know one, is another good way to choose the path of least resistance. And obviously, if either parent or nearby grandparent is a native speaker of a world-class language, that's the one to learn. The pleasant associations of learning a language from a loved one go a long way toward taking the sting out of the first steps.

If you don't have any language in your reserve of knowledge, your two best bets are French and German. French is probably the best choice. France has a world-class literature that peaked in the nineteenth century, recent enough that the masterpieces are readily understandable and relevant to modern sensibility. And while you would never know it by the amount of attention given to Parisian fads and fashions, France produces enough hightech aircraft, avionics, and scientific information so that even boys, who are not much interested in perfume and lingerie, will find plenty to fascinate them.

German is my second choice for several reasons. German, like French, has a world-class literature that peaked in the nineteenth century, and many German masterworks are still of great interest. An added advantage is that many of the best German writers, including Johannes Wolfgang von Goethe, Friedrich Schiller, and Heinrich Heine, wrote some of their works *im Volkston,* meaning in simple language. Even a first-year student can read the works of great poets in the original German. Above all, the German language offers the folktales of the Brothers Grimm, which most children have already learned to love in English translation. France, of course, offers the fairy tales of Charles Perrault, also splendid examples of telling stories with a bold plot and a simple vocabulary. An enormous benefit of German is that many of the simple words are *cognates*—the same spellings as their English equivalents, or close enough so that even a child can recognize them. This familiarity is also true of many French words, which is the reason why I recommend one or the other language as the ideal starter language.

Italian and Spanish offer fewer cognates. Italian, however, is an extremely beautiful language, and a strong contender for the attention of anyone who shows an affinity for music or art. Spanish offers a consistent and easy pronunciation, an impressive cultural heritage including the works of Miguel Cervantes and Lope de Vega, and readily available literature in Spanish and bilingual editions. The hemispheric importance of Spanish spoken in all the major American countries except for the United States, Canada, and Brazil, is staggering. Spanish is already the second language of the United States.

Other languages may also be considered, especially the so-called "strategic languages"—Russian, Arabic, Chinese, and Japanese—which are spoken by relatively few native-born Americans. But learning any of these four is so difficult that it's probably better not to spring them on kids unless you have a native speaker in the family and plenty of handy instructional material.

Let's say you've picked French, but you don't speak French yourself. What do you do now?

The first thing you do is go out and buy a paperback book, *See It and Say It in French,* by Margarita Madrigal. This book is available in most bigger bookstores. If they don't have it in stock, they can certainly order it.

The idea of this book is to teach you French the way children learn it, by associating simple, frequently repeated phrases with pictures. One of the best ways to broach this subject to younger children is to pretend that you're going on a voyage to France and want to *prepare* by learning the language. (It's nice, of course, if you can somehow set aside the time and money to make an actual trip to France, or to Quebec, but children have wonderful imaginations, and a *pretend* voyage to France will get you through the initial stages of resistance to the language almost as well as the real thing. You can spice up the lesson, if you want, with snacks from the country you are studying. Johnny used to get a tremendous kick out of putting on a beret and having a croissant with milk during or before his French lesson. The way he dramatized eating that croissant showed he was acquiring a taste for French culture.

Don't try to push through *See It and Say It in French* in a few sittings. It's best to do the first lesson on the first day; then go over the first lesson on the second day, before plowing into the second lesson. The lessons are a few pages each, with a few repetitive sentences on each page. But you have to build a solid base by making sure that the child remembers all, or at least most, of the words before moving on to the next lesson. One of the reasons that Americans often hate foreign languages is that they learn things *not* to know and remember them, but to pass tests in them. You can't learn a language that way, because if you don't know every form of the verbs *is* and *has,* it's pointless to learn the vocabulary further on in the book. You have to build on a rock, not on sand. This is one of the reasons why you should start children learning their first foreign language by the time they are six or seven. It may take the child three times as long to learn the language, but once the younger child learns the basics, the retention will be excellent. My daughter, who started under protest at the age of five, can't remember a time when she could not read basic French or German, or had any trouble with the pronunciations. She might not be able to give a word-for-word translation of Marcel Proust or Thomas Mann in the original, but she can pick up the newspaper in either language and give you the gist of any story with near-perfect accuracy. From this point on, study of complex literature in senior high school or college is fairly easy. But I pity anybody who tries to decipher Proust or Mann after starting French or German in college.

Take your time with *See It and Say It* ... in whatever language. (The book also has editions that handle German, Italian, and Spanish.) I would not attempt to offer lessons of more than 10 or 15 minutes at first. Even after the child begins to remember the words, I would not drag introductory lessons out for more than 15 minutes for the first year. You want the child to like the language, not hate it.

Fun is a vital part of every lesson. When you get to the part of the book where the various foods are named, you can have a French feast. Match the foods pictured in the book with the ones on the table. Then let the child ask for the food by name in French. They love doing this.

You can expand the game around the house. Go to the closet and let the child find the foreign names of clothing. He or she can tell you what the names are. Or you can point and let the child guess. Use the book as a reference.

Children seem to have an instinctive love of toys. It's almost as if they need to have a little world of their own that they can control until they get some leverage in the big world. You can benefit the child enormously if you turn that love of toys into a love of language.

Round up some low-cost, unbreakable toys that are big enough to be easily visible, but not so big that they encroach on your living space. The size I found best was the standard military-miniature size of 54 mm—the size where a human figure is about three inches tall. Most drug-store toys come in this size. You can get a collection of farm animals, zoo animals, cowboys and Indians, or soldiers at $2 to $4 per bag. The whole toy armada may cost $10—less, if you shop around. Having gathered up these toys, to the delight of the child, you set them up and ask him or her to name them in French. You can make a game of this activity by letting the child keep any toy he or she can name. The child develops a tactile stimulation from handling the toys and a sense of competition from seeing how many he or she can name.

You can also ask the child questions once you've learned a few phrases yourself: Which one is brown? Which one is white? Which one is biggest? Smallest? Youngest? Oldest?

Believe it or not, the hardest part is over. Now the child can name objects, answer questions, and play games in French—or any other language you may have chosen.

Now it's time for another book and another step. The step is understanding written stories in French. The book is *Fun with French* by Lee Cooper.

Ms. Cooper performed a tremendous service when she wrote or co-authored the books in this series: *Fun with French, Fun with German, Fun with Italian, Fun with Spanish,* and even *More Fun with Spanish,* actually live up to their names. They really do make it fun to teach these languages to children.

The books trade heavily on cognates—words that are the same or similar in English and in the language being learned. The first chapter carries a pronunciation guide. But the key to the importance of the *Fun with . . .* books is that the pictures illustrate the stories, but don't completely explain them. An adult, however, can easily understand the stories, and so can a child with an adult's help. The books are all too short, but they also feature games to be played in learning the languages. Each book also has a glossary. Some of them are out of print, but you can find the *Fun with . . .* books in most children's libraries.

Again, it's important not to push too hard. One story per day is right for the first sortee into the books. Build up by doing the previous day's story before you do a new one. What I did was to take each book out of the library a few times. The first time I went through the book step-by-step. The next time, Emily and later Johnny was so glad to see the "old friend" again that the book was read without any pushing. And another few hundred words entered the child's vocabulary.

Now the fun really began. Once the *Fun with . . .* book was mastered, Emily discovered she could actually read simple stories in French. We combed area libraries to find suitable books. Most children's libraries actually will have four or five books in either French or Spanish on hand at any given time. In urban areas, of course, or in affluent communities, the selection will be larger. It was a lot of fun, and a great excuse to get the kids into the library, where many other experiences were also available. The kids were also happy with this activity because the foreign language books gave them a chance to read the sort of large-print, large-picture books their age-mates were reading. The difference was that the age-mates were reading the picture books in English while Emily (and later Johnny) read them in French and German. By this time, their English-level ability had progressed to the point where they were reading juvenile biographies and science and history books in English. Foreign languages gave them a toehold in superior reading skills they would otherwise have relinquished during childhood.

Now it's time to go multimedia. You and the child have plowed through the basics of French and learned a number of words. But what does the language actually sound like?

Records and tapes are widely available to teach you how to say basic words and phrases. These investments are good, but it's better not to overdo it at first. The child should learn the language gradually, without turning it into a grind. One of the best aids I found, while teaching both Emily and Johnny, was a record called "Lucienne Vernay Sings Songs in French for Children" (Columbia Masterworks). The record contains an artful mixture of traditional French songs and cheery 1950s Disney-types, including "Who's Afraid of the Big Bad Wolf" in French. Vernay's clear singing voice and careful pronunciation make the record a joy for both teacher and student to listen to. The record comes with a song sheet, illustrated with simple drawings, in which the French lyrics are set down side by side with an English translation. I would recommend one step: Take the song sheet to a copy shop and have it enlarged 150 or 200 percent. Children hate small print, and unless their eyes are destined to be nearsighted, they have trouble reading it. An enlarged copy will make it easier to get them to concentrate on the words while they listen to the music.

A number of other records feature the same possibilities. I recommend Vernay because I had great success with her record. But the children's department of your own record store or library may contain others just as good.

The amateur historian, of course, can have a lot of fun explaining to his children why the words of the songs are not always as innocent as they seem. The translation of one song, *"As-Tu Vu la Casquette de père Bugeaud?"* is given as "Have You Seen the Cap of the Old Man?" What it really means, of course, is "Have You Seen the Cap of Father Bugeaud?" Father Bugeaud was the old Napoleonic general who later subdued Algeria for France in the 1830s. The fact that the melody of the song is the French military bugle call for *Assembly* ought to be a tip-off to kids who watch Foreign Legion movies. (Since part of Emily's and Johnny's cultural enrichment was watching the classic 1939 black-and-white version of *Beau Geste,* the point wasn't lost on them. Of this, more later.)

Once the home schooler has begun to actually speak and sing in French, it's time to make a thorough survey of the basic language. There is a superb book available for this task but you may have to look hard to find it. The book is *Mon Premier Dictionnaire* by Roger Pillet, who was the chairman of the Foreign Language Department, Laboratory School, University of Chicago. *Mon Premier Dictionnaire* was published in 1963 and has been officially out of print for much of the past two decades, but it's a vital tool in expanding French from the beginner level to literacy. You can probably find one in any large children's library. When you do, you may want to take it out for an extended loan.

Mon Premier Dictionnaire (My First Dictionary) defines the 2,400 most important words in French—entirely in the original language. The definitions include simple sentences, small quotes, and about 1,000 color illustrations. The child who has gone through *See It and Say It* and the Lee Cooper book with its heavy reliance on cognates will find *Mon Premier Dictionnaire* to be good mental exercise, but not an insurmountable challenge.

The best way to handle *Mon Premier Dictionnaire* is slowly but surely. Start off doing about two pages a day, every day, side by side with the child. You may find that the child resists the learning experience for the first couple of dozen pages— "this is hard"—and you'll want to keep an eye on the book at all times so the child doesn't arrange to lose it for you. However, if you can persist to the end of the first hundred pages, you'll see something remarkable: the child will not only stop resisting, but actually begin to go through whole definitions by himself or herself. By the end of the dictionary—*zero* on page 457—you and your home schooler should have discovered two striking facts: French is not really all that different from English once you master the basics: and learning a European language is a lot easier and more fun than you thought it would be.

The good news is that once you and your home schooler have completely learned the vocabulary in *Mon Premier Dictionnaire,* you will know enough French to actually read the language itself.

You will not, of course, have mastered the book the first time you plow through it. The best plan is to go through it once, then review it a second time—and perhaps a third. This process sounds tedious, but you will find that younger children don't resent tedium as much as teenagers do—another reason that it's better to start foreign languages at five, six, or seven than in high school, where the time and patience needed to memorize get lost between dating and sports.

What do you give the children to read? Some larger or older library children's rooms will have extensive collections of works in French, and also in German. Failing that, you may want to check the adult section of the library for easy-reading books in French, often intended for high school or college courses. These books will probably contain selections of French writing chosen for their simple vocabularies that a beginner can read without much trouble.

If your interest and dedication become as serious as I think they will, you may want to order books from Alliance Francaise or the French and Spanish Book Store, both located in New York City. These outlets can supply you with lists or catalogs of French children's books, juvenile books, and other publications.

One book I would particularly recommend is *L'Histoire de France* (The Story of France) by Philippe Brochard, with original illustrations by Pierre Brochard, published by Editions Fernand Nathan in 1984. This large-format, handsome book, with original art in color and many reproduced period paintings and photographs, offers a look at French history from prehistoric and Roman times to the 1980s, with a reasonable degree of objectivity. The vocabulary is such that a home schooler, who has finished *Mon Premier Dictionnaire*, will be able to make his or her way through with understanding—and a dictionary. (I once showed a copy of this book to a college sophomore who had taken four years of French in high school plus two in college, and he asked to borrow the book. He didn't have any trouble with the vocabulary. He just wanted to brush up on the facts—and enjoy the pictures. It's a fine book to give someone as a reward for completing *Mon Premier Dictionnaire.*)

Televised courses are also available on PBS that are worth

a look. My children enjoyed *"Parlez-Moi"* (Speak to Me) when they were kindergarten age. This short, Canadian-made series features Sol the Clown in amusing adventures, repeated bit by bit with English explanations and basic words spelled out so that any child who is basically able to read can develop a feel for French pronunciation. On a somewhat more mature level, *"À Vous La France"* (France for You) teaches high school and adult students about modern French life and customs while exploring the basics of the language. Neither show is a substitute for book work, but both are a good addition to a course that sets aside 15 to 30 minutes per day for side-by-side instruction.

PBS also offers courses in German, Italian, Spanish, Russian, and Greek. I know because my kids insisted that we watch and tape all of them. The German course, *"Deutsch Direkt"* became a vital part of Johnny's lessons. My daughter also made extensive use of *"Buongiorno Italia"* and *"Zarabanda,"* the Italian and Spanish shows, especially to sharpen her pronunciation.

Some of the benefits of learning a major foreign language as a child are intangible. I remember we were once taking Johnny through George Washington's Headquarters in Morristown, New Jersey. The only other people on the tour were four Germans, who gazed around politely, meanwhile talking German to one another a mile a minute. The tour guide, a college student originally from North Carolina, didn't have the slightest idea what they were talking about. He wasn't sure whether they were appreciating the Ford Mansion or plotting a takeover. Johnny, who was then 8, formed an instant affinity for the guide, who looked about 16 and was obviously nervous.

"Don't worry," he said furtively. "I'll translate for you."

The guide looked somewhat surprised and wasn't sure whether or not to take Johnny seriously—until the eight-year-old *interpreter* began to supply him with a running account of what the four Germans thought of Washington's Headquarters.

"They wonder if people were smaller then than they are now," Johnny said at one point. The guide, who knew his stuff and clearly loved history, launched into a description of people's sizes in the eighteenth century in English. The Germans seemed surprised that he had picked up on their conversation. Johnny kept mum except when he had the guide's ear to himself.

By the time the tour was over, everybody—the Germans, the guide, Johnny, and I—had had a delightful time. Finally one of the Germans came over and—having spotted the *interpreter* in action when he became careless—asked him a direct question.

"They want to take our picture," Johnny told the guide.

The two of them posed outside the Ford family bedroom, and again on the steps of the mansion. The world will little note nor long remember that afternoon, but I think everybody there was touched with friendship and understanding. And I know I was a very proud father.

The other benefits are more practical. Foreign languages are said to boost SAT scores by 100 points or more. They can lead directly to jobs that involve higher pay and travel. They can also interest college admissions officers who have long since come to regard most native-born Americans as hopelessly monolingual. Many a college admissions officer will overlook the mediocrity of a high school, or of a high school transcript with Bs and Cs on it if the student applying for admission can demonstrate an ability to speak and read French or German. Even if your child's school is doing a completely adequate job of teaching English and math, it is well worth the time to snap off a less-than-favorite TV show for a half hour every night and pick up *See It and Say It* . . . and the Lee Cooper book on your language of choice. Your child may not think so at the age of six, but, believe me, it's one of the enrichments she or he will be most grateful for in high school and college. But that's not when you should start to teach French or German. The best time is right now.

FOUR

Every Day Is Enrichment Day

Have you ever watched a grade school field trip in progress?

I confess that every time I see one coming, I give it the widest possible berth. I treat it rather as I would treat a tornado or a buffalo stampede—as something that's fascinating to watch from a safe distance.

I will confess that I took part in these rampages myself, and not only as a kid. The first year that Emily returned to public school in fifth grade, the kids made a trip to Philadelphia. I didn't get to go on that one. I think I was hiding. The bus took off from the school at 9 A.M., spent three hours on the road, most of it stuck in traffic, and returned at 4:30 P.M., also after three hours in traffic. The mathematically inclined reader will note that the children got to spend an hour and a half in the city of Brotherly Love—and six hours in the bus. This experience was certainly educational. It taught the children how to ride a bus.

The sixth-grade trip was aimed at the Bronx Zoo. I volunteered for this safari for two reasons: I love the zoo, and I wanted to make sure none of her friends would lure Emily out of the iron fence for an excursion into the mean streets of the Bronx, where she might disappear forever.

The teacher and the class mothers were glad to have me

along. A large, nasty-looking man with a beard is not the worst thing to take with you on a trip to the Bronx. The trip was also an education for me. These suburban kids didn't strangle one another with the rolling bus windows or throw things at the people on the streets, which is what I remembered my classmates doing during school trips 25 years before. Some of them actually seemed interested in the animals — almost as interested as they were in the food, the souvenirs, and sparring or gossiping with the same kids they saw in class every school day of the year.

Field trips are fun. They're supposed to be fun. But what they're really supposed to be about is education. Are they educational? I venture to say many students east of the Mississippi have been to Washington, D.C., Boston, or Philadelphia to visit the sites where American independence first became a reality. The test scores across the nation reveal that today's students, including those from Massachusetts, Pennsylvania, and the District of Columbia, know far less about the leaders, the battles, and the issues of the American Revolution than what the farm children in a Kansas schoolhouse at the turn of the century did. Seeing all the sights doesn't count for much if you don't know what you are looking at.

I think it's a good idea to take the kids out of the stuffy classroom and the noisy halls every couple of days — not once a year — but I think it's a serious mistake to tie up a whole day busing them across the state to a site they won't remember when the main attraction is the fast food in the refreshment stand and the teacher is too busy keeping track of stragglers to explain anything.

The idea of the field trip brings the idea of enrichment into focus. School is a lot more fun today than it was 25 or 50 years ago. Students in the lower grades are exposed not only to lecturers but singers, dancers, clowns, puppeteers, and people who talk about what it's like to be a brain surgeon or a firefighter. Some of these lectures may prompt the students to read up on the subjects. Some of them may even take up careers on the basis of the lectures, though trying to make a living as a singer, dancer, clown, or puppeteer is an unenviable experience unless you're an absolute genius with a streak of wonderful good luck. The real problem is that the schools tend to pick these lectures out of catalogs based on what's available. Worse still, all the *enrichment* takes class time and attention away from the part of school that is absolutely vital: reading and math.

Consider what you can do with *enrichment* as part of your own school program:

In the first place, you are not constrained to pick the talent as if you were ordering from a menu. You can select anything in your town, your county, or any nearby city that admits children, if you can afford the time and money. You can take the child to something that is a night or weekend activity. Best of all, perhaps, you can use the field trip to spend quality time with your child that educators and psychologists are always talking about. And you'll find that when you have one, two, or even three children with you instead of a whole wolfpack of fighting, weeping, wandering, bored, or whining tourists, you can actually explain things and use the field trip for educational enrichment and not for just a breath of fresh air.

A guide at the Bergen County Wildlife Center, a few miles from my house, summed it up nicely: If you're roaming through the woods looking for deer or hawks, don't do it with a second-grade class trip of 30 noisy, tangle-footed seven-year-olds. Do it with one adult and one, or at most, two children. That's true whether you're stalking a deer or a great Renaissance painting.

The idea of combining field trips with your own personal tastes has one pitfall. The adult's tastes tend to vector the adult into whatever the adult finds interesting such as sports or shopping. The trouble with this approach is that most schools already overemphasize sports to the detriment of academics. Some kids in junior high school and high school care about nothing else, until they discover cars and the opposite sex. Ironically, the boys, who traditionally become the bread-winners, are the "sports nuts" who fritter away four to six years of high school on the practice field or in the gym while they ignore the library. The girls, who have traditionally ex-pected, or at least hoped, that men would support them and their children, are the ones who take part in the literary, dramatic, and musical events that tend to build verbal skills and encourage reading. The schools should try to reverse this trend in every way they can, short of producing a nation of sports-crazy Amazon women and effete boys who can't catch a basketball. Right now there's no danger of that hap-pening. Top athletes have been enlisted, especially among minority groups, to warn kids that professional sports don't provide many jobs. Reading and math skills, on the other hand, are vital to economic survival in the world of Life After Graduation. But it's still up to parents who love their children to explain, calmly and firmly, that sports are strictly recre-ational and have nothing whatsoever to do with school's core purpose, which is to teach reading, writing, math, and more advanced skills. For this reason, the home-supplementing parent cannot consider a spectator sports event to be any kind of academic enrichment.

The classic field trip, of course, is to the art museum. Nothing brings history alive like seeing the real thing—stat-ues, paintings, armor, weapons, tools, pottery, and jewelry of the peoples of the past. Any child who finds this experience boring simply hasn't been prepared for it.

I'll explain with a personal example. When Emily was in the sixth grade and Johnny was still studying at home, we *did* the Metropolitan Museum of Art for the first time. I'm not crazy about driving into New York City. More particularly, I'm not crazy about leaving my car parked there. A substan-tial number of people outside the city share this feeling, and that's probably why most suburban libraries have bus tours to the Met once or twice a year. For $12 to $15, you can reserve a seat and skip tolls, parking, gasoline, and parking tickets that could easily cost you twice as much.

The bus trip was announced almost a month before departure, and since Johnny was not in school and bound to a set curriculum, I had plenty of time to get him ready. My intention was to get as much out of the trip as I could, so I got large illustrated books about Egypt, Greece, and Rome out of the library. I also set up a tape of *Moulin Rouge,* John Huston's classic 1950s film about the life of Henri de Toulouse-Lautrec. (Some readers may find this film's implied sexuality rather gamy fare for an eight-year-old, but you can see a lot worse on most prime-time or cable stations.) The next two weeks were spent scanning the TV listings, and we found another score—a PBS special, mixing cartoons and diagrams with actual photography, about the building of the pyramids.

The day arrived. We rode the bus to the Metropolitan Museum of Art and arrived on Fifth Avenue in a light snowfall. I paid $5 and the kids got in free.

Right after we got through the lobby, Johnny locked onto target.

"Wow, man! An Egyptian tomb!"

He was off like a flash, and before I could catch him, he had charged into the maze-like tomb like a bat.

"Aha! The canopic jars!" Johnny exclaimed. He was Howard Carter or Lord Carnovan by now, explaining the tomb to me, to his sister, several children he had never seen before, and their bus driver, a man from Hungary, as I later found out, named Attila.

"The first step in the mummification process is to excise the viscera," Johnny explained to his audience with terse precision. "The excised viscera are stored in the canopic jars. This one's for the heart, this one's for the lungs. They discarded the brain after it had been excised, because they didn't know it was good for anything. After that, the body was steeped in natron for 70 days. Natron is a bituminous salt. . . ."

The other children didn't know exactly what to make of Johnny. Neither did Attila, the bus driver.

"How old is this boy?" he asked in a Bela Lugosi accent.
"Just turned eight," I said.

"Eight!" he said with surprise. "Then he is *genius!* At first
I thought he was *midget.*"

Johnny rampaged around the Egyptian wing of the Met,
awed by finding the indoor Temple of Dendur. When we
roamed through the Roman wing, he marveled at the chariot,
and paused before the helmets, wondering how large or small
the people might have been. The statues, especially the huge
Hercules, made an enormous impression on him. But when
we entered the second floor, past the extensive collections of
pottery to the section where the nineteenth-century paintings were kept, my foresight paid off.

"Wow! Look at this!" he gasped. "There really *was* a *Moulin Rouge!*" He was gazing at some of the paintings he had
seen in the film version.

"I saw him paint this!" he told Attila and the guard.

"This boy is remarkable," Attila told me.

Alphonse de Neuville's big painting of *Friedland,* with Napoleon's army formed for battle, brought about another explo-
sion of detailed commentary.

"There's Napoleon. That looks like Marshal Ney. Those
guys in the background are, I'd say, the Middle Guard, because they don't look old enough to be the Old Guard. The
cavalrymen in green are Chasseurs. The guys in blue with
the steel armor are Cuirassiers. I guess they've already started-
ed fighting because that cannon's got a wheel missing. . . ."

Emily enjoyed the museum in a less spectacular way. She
was fascinated by the jewelry, and paused thoughtfully before
the paintings, examining them closer or farther to see how
the perspective changed the image. But what impressed me
was how much Johnny, a fleet-footed fugitive from piano lessons if ever there was one, actually got out of the Metropolitan Museum of Art. Neither Emily nor Johnny was ready to
leave when the time came. They vowed they would be
back—and they have been, repeatedly.

In cultural terms, the Met is a big deal—one of the biggest

in the world. But there are many smaller deals in our own backyard, within a 10-minute ride, that can be visited as a special reward if the day's lessons are finished early.

The field trip we take most often is to the Bergen County Wildlife Center in Wyckoff, about five minutes from our home. My wife and I make a point of getting the children there at least once with each changing season, and in the summer we probably go there once or twice a month.

This park features a field house with exhibits that change every few months. Nature and science films are shown twice a week, and there is a sort of zoo consisting of those animals that once roamed wild in the Northeast. The animals in the cages, incidentally, are mostly road-crippled creatures that have recovered enough to be put on display but would not survive in the wild. The Wildlife Center also has a small lake that attracts 20 different species of wild ducks, geese, and other waterfowl.

As a family, one of our favorite features is the nature trail, about a half-mile long, that rambles through five or six different habitats, ranging from hardwood forest to rocky pine slopes to meadow to swamp. Boardwalks cover the muddiest places, and the marginal sections have enough gravel or shredded bark on the trail so you won't ruin a good pair of shoes. The trees and shrubs are numbered on signs, and you can pick up a trail guide—a piece of paper with the names and facts about the trees listed by number. We take the guided tour about once a year, and the rest of the time we just hike for exercise and relaxation.

Just one town away, in Franklin Lakes, there is the Audubon Society Center. The concept here is the same, except that the emphasis is on bird-watching, the exhibits in the field house are different, the trail is a little shorter, but almost as varied, and the gift shop sells a variety of books and educational toys and games.

Within 10 minutes we use another asset—the Bergen County Museum of Art and Science in Paramus. This museum, located on the ground floor of a three-story mansion, features more nature exhibits. But there's also a recreation room in which children can play science-oriented games with mirrors and weights, optical illusions, and static electricity. Play, in fact, is encouraged in some parts of this museum, which is a welcome change from the "don't touch" policy of most other galleries. The Bergen County Museum also features two mastodon skeletons, one of them assembled and the other shown *in situ,* as it was discovered in a nearby town.

Bergen County, like most suburbs, is heavily dependent on the nearest big city, in this case New York City, for major cultural attractions. But you can make a number of worthwhile educational field trips in 10 minutes of driving or less.

The commitment has to be there. You can't expect any school to educate your child effectively, no matter how dedicated the teachers are and how hard they try, unless you are willing to turn off prime-time TV and turn on your imagination. You've also got to take time out from shopping and paid sports events. The fringe benefit, of course, is that most cultural events that admit children are far less expensive than the paid attractions conducted for profit. Many are free. You will actually save money—maybe hundreds of dollars a year—if you break the "paid entertainment" habit and learn to appreciate museums, zoos, and those historic homes that offer tours.

Some places are out there waiting to be discovered. Some events occur on a regular schedule. On the East Coast, the focus of most historic events is the American Revolution. Farther west, the topic may be the Indian Wars, the growth of national industries, the Old West, or the meeting of English-speaking cultures with people of French, Spanish, or Asian heritage. What all this rhetoric translates to is a good time for the kids and for the parents—and a wonderful educational opportunity.

People have all sorts of hobbies. Some race cars, some hang glide, and some hunt or fish. But the hobbyists that every home schooling parent should feel grateful for are those "reenactors" who spend hundreds or thousands of dollars on costumes and equipment, and then drive dozens, even hundreds of miles on weekends to attend colonial, Civil War, or Wild West fairs, or American Indian powwows. If your child or children have any interest at all in history or literature, or even if they enjoy the costumed characters in picture books, they'll go semiwild with excitement at the sight of soldiers in Continental and British uniforms skirmishing, of Civil War encampments, or of American Indians in full regalia dancing and setting up tepees. These events crop up annually, sometimes more often, at select locations. The Steuben House in River Edge and Jockey Hollow in Morristown are the two usual assembly points for colonial events on a large scale in northern New Jersey.

In one of the towns that borders ours, Fair Lawn, the Garretson Forge & Farm Restoration features several get-togethers each year in which the Outwater Militia camp out in all kinds of weather, wearing uniforms or civilian clothing from the time of George Washington. Costumed soldiers load and fire their muskets, cast musket balls out of hot lead, and cook beef and chickens over an open fire—sometimes in the middle of snowstorms. The group even has its own Indian— actually an Italian-American schoolteacher, but his respect and affection for American Indian culture is so sincere that nobody resents the ethnic line-crossing. They have their own blacksmith, Alexander John, a retired engineer who's past 80 but still swings a mean hammer. Linda Russell, a colonial balladeer who works at federal buildings in New York City, often comes out to sing and play the sort of music that Americans knew and loved in the days of George Washington—and lets the children help perform. There's no better way to bring the supposedly starchy figures of the American Revolution to life than to listen to Ms. Russell's ballads and dance music on authentic instruments.

Another fine entertainer, who specializes in the Civil War, is Bobby Horton, of Birmingham, Alabama, a sixth-generation descendant of Confederate veterans. Perhaps the ultimate one-man band, Bobby records Civil War music, North and South, performing the parts himself and blending them on an eight-track system. The sound is so authentic that he received a favorable review in *American Heritage,* which has exact standards for accuracy. His voice and performance has just the right blend of sentiment, wit, and raucous vitality to revive an important era. There's nothing better to play in the car's tape deck when you're driving to a Civil War site or reenactment.

One sure way to assure your kids a warm welcome at these events is to come in costume. This isn't as expensive as it sounds. You can either rent a costume — usually $25 or so — or, perhaps better for purposes of budget and learning, make a costume if somebody in the family sews. You can buy one outright if you're a hard-core enthusiast for any particular era. Or you can improvise one out of hand-me-downs, leftovers, or clothes picked up from a thrift shop. The amount of stitchery in a girl's colonial dress is negligible. If the girl is still under 10, she can get by in a pinch by throwing a large shawl over a cotton slip or bundling a flannel robe round her waist with a sash. Check out picture books to see how this looks.

You can fake a boy's colonial costume by finding a white shirt a few sizes too big, sewing up the front, and tightening the cuffs to make the sleeves billow out. Over the shirt he can wear a dark solid-color vest. For breeches, you can use football-style pants, or cut away an old pair of snug trousers at the knee. High white socks and dark loafers complete the lower part of the costume.

For the girl's hat, you can use a big straw hat with the widest possible brim, or a sunbonnet, or no hat at all. The boy can wear a standard wide-brimmed cowboy hat, with no crease on the top. If he's aiming for fashion, he can pin up either one side or all three corners of the brim. That's how the three-corner hat got its start in the seventeenth century, long before George Washington and George III.

Cowboy costumes are even easier for boys. A light solid-color shirt, a dark vest, and that same cowboy hat, minus the pins, and he has it made. What do cowboys wear below the belt? Blue jeans. And prairie skirts and blouses for girls are not hard to locate.

You will be amazed to see how getting dressed up in a Revolutionary War or Wild West costume dramatizes the era and the people that lived in that era, and makes it easier to get the child to read about it.

There's a big difference between forcing the kid to read five books on the American Revolution, or the Civil War, or the Old West, and giving him or her the chance to research his or her own costume and character for a share in a pageant to make that era visible. One reading assignment is a chore. The other is an open door to excitement and enjoyment. If you were a kid, which would you rather do? Read because a grown-up says so, or prepare for a magical trip to the colorful past?

And that's what enrichment is all about.

Opportunities are available to take your children to museums, science exhibits, historic sites, and scenes of great natural beauty in every county of the United States. Big cities may be more richly endowed with major museums, but if you check out the local newspapers you will discover that there's something interesting occurring within a half-hour's drive of most homes any weekend. Large newspapers run calendars of coming events. Libraries provide announcements in the form of notices and brochures. You can also visit the county seat and see what is available in terms of landmarks. Once you plug into the network of historic and cultural events, you may be tapped to work as a volunteer, or even solicited for money. But you won't lack for things to do or places to go.

Once a year, the town fathers, in their wisdom, allow young people to take over part of a council meeting. At least half of these meetings are punctuated by protests from high school seniors—supposedly the best and brightest kids in their schools—that "there's nothing to do in these towns."

What these kids think they're saying is "How bored we

are!" What they're really saying is "How boring we are!"

The schools have peer-grouped their imaginations to death. Through constantly emphasizing comformity and age-adjusted-to-the-norm learning, the schools have convinced them that they can only associate with people their own ages. And they've convinced them that the only activities that have any meaning have to revolve around sports, dances, and "hangin' out" with people as much like themselves as humanly possible. No wonder they're bored.

Within 15 minutes' drive of the towns where these poor kids have nothing to do, I've taken my children to three wildlife centers we visit on a regular basis. I've taken them on a tour of a U.S. fleet-type submarine, a historic airport control tower that has been turned into a museum, two miniature zoos, a working farm with beehives, a sheep-shearing, five or six colonial events, an Indian powwow, an air show featuring biplanes of the 1920s and 1930s, several events involving vintage automobiles, an opera gala with stars from the Metropolitan Opera, a poetry reading by William Wordsworth's great-great-grand-nephew, a newspaper plant with printing operations in full progress, art sessions with painters doing portraits of (clothed) models, outdoor and indoor art shows, and various nature walks conducted within a few blocks of my own home. This list doesn't include trips to New York City, West Point, or any of the other national sites of importance within an hour's drive. Nor does it consider church-related events, including pony rides, hay rides, vigils, and other religious or social events. And when all else fails, there's always the library, where books, tapes, records, and computers can take anyone with a little imagination almost anywhere—if he or she once learns that reading can be enjoyed.

The irony is that, while the kids being processed like potatoes in high school think there is nothing to do, all sorts of church, civil, and historical groups struggle because they can not get enough volunteers—and because the teenagers are not interested. The mass mentality of the schools and their peer-grouping has turned the teenaged rebels into such conformists that few of them would be caught dead taking part in group activities that include adults, seniors, and younger children. Yet teenagers who do get involved in volunteer work, either with churches or with civic groups, are not only insulated from the follow-the-herd mentality that leads to drug abuse, they're already building a network that may lead to future employment or academic success.

The single greatest enrichment you can offer your son or daughter is the idea that he or she does not *hafta* do what everybody else does—which may, in a few short years, mean doing drugs, getting involved in precocious sexual activities, or even in gang violence. These aren't *rebel* activities— they're conformist activities among kids in the wrong peer group. Mass-processed kids bore themselves into drug abuse and precocious sex because they're too chicken to break with the herd and discover the real pleasures of a developing adult intelligence and a Christian perspective. The youngster who turns an interest in science, art, or history into a network that includes responsible, moral adults as well as bright, like-minded teenagers with similar interests is truly enriched— and truly insulated from the lemminglike instinct for self-destruction that seems to fuel so many less fortunate teenagers.

FIVE

Testing Your Progress

This chapter will be a short one. Public schools spend so much time and effort on testing that I think home teachers should be contrarians and test a lot less—but a lot more effectively.

The horror stories don't need much repeating because most parents have heard them. The simple fact is that those students who *are* academically oriented or intellectually competitive spend so much time preparing for tests, taking tests, and worrying about tests before, during and after the tests that they barely have time to learn anything but how to pass tests.

A major case in point is the Scholastic Aptitude Tests, or SATs, which play a big role in determining who gets into what college. The SATs originated when college administrators faced a problem brought on by regionalized schools: Kids who received straight A's all through high school sometimes entered college unable to read, spell, punctuate, or do simple math. Some public schools seemed to award academic A's for perfect attendance, without bothering to keep track of how many class hours the student stayed awake. Especially in the inner cities, many schools still grade by this formula.

The writers of the SATs bowed in this direction by awarding an automatic 200 points to any kid who shows up for the test and finds the place to write his or her name, both in the math and verbal test. Since the maximum score is 1600, examinees are 400 points toward their goal just by plunking their posteriors on their chairs. The rest of the test is based on vocabulary, logic, and math skills that range from basic to fairly advanced at the secondary level.

SATs can, in fact, weed out any student who's completely illiterate or has a serious math problem. If you don't know the times tables and a little simple geometry, you won't do well in the math department either. The tests don't measure cultural literacy, creativity, or a lot of other things that go into making a first-rate mind. But because SATs are important to college admissions, and potentially important to winning scholarships, some parents turn them into the Greatest Show on Earth—or an Americanized version of what the Japanese call *Examination Hell.* A cottage industry has emerged, where professional educators spend their nights and weekends running cram courses in which students are taught how to take the tests effectively and are force-fed the kind of information they should have picked up gradually through assigned and recreational reading.

Youngsters can now earn the right to take SATs in the seventh grade if they do well on the California Tests, which screen out students who can't read before puberty. Those who score high enough receive a preview of coming attractions. My daughter, Emily, scored straight 99s in all the important academic areas of the California Achievement Tests and earned the right to take the SATs early. I was tremendously impressed—until my wife discovered that almost a *third* of Emily's seventh-grade classmates had achieved similar honors, including some who were not notably gifted and still had what I would regard as serious problems in basic skills.

Clearly, American schools are test-happy. And the kids are slap-happy. The following is a sample of a question in a social studies test given for academic credit: "What was the importance of youth movements in the recent history of Nigeria?"

Here's a question from an amateur historian: How many children will remember the answer to that question two weeks after the test is completed and handed in?

Some home schoolers probably get roped into the institutional fantasy. They think home school is not a real school unless they give real tests. If the home school student doesn't have nightmares and get cold sweats and stomach cramps, the home school teacher feels she or he is not doing the job.

Wrong! The purpose of testing is not to give the kids headaches or upset stomachs. Nor are tests supposed to force the kids to cram their memories full of facts they never learned before and will never need or want to know again.

There is only one purpose for testing: To find out if the child knows everything he or she is supposed to know, or if he or she needs help to learn more.

Your best test is the day-to-day progress of the child's lessons. When you're reading with him or her side by side, it's too early to begin formal testing. But you've already begun the remediation that formal testing sometimes points up the need for. If the child stumbles over a word, you help. If the child doesn't know what a word means, you explain it.

The same is true in the early stages of math. The test comes when the child fills out the answers. If the child knows what he or she is supposed to know, the child doesn't need to be tested as part of your home or supplemental program. If he or she doesn't, you see that the child learns it, immediately, without making him or her feel like a failure. For instance, if the child constantly gets 6 x 7 wrong in the times tables, you ask him or her to recite it 20 times. Check the child the next day and make sure he or she knows it. If the child doesn't, start over. This procedure should not be presented as punishment, and you should *never* spank or slap the child or call him or her stupid, no matter how many times the child makes the same mistake. But you should make sure that the child learns not to keep making the same mistakes.

By working side by side with the child on a daily basis, for at least one hour, better two, you will learn to know exactly what his or her strengths and weaknesses are and to provide personalized corrections. This activity is even easier if you are one of those fortunate parents who can afford to home school the child on a full-time basis, though, given the economic facts of life, most parents can't.

Whether your child is being educated supplementally or schooled full-time at home, there are better ways than a formal test to evaluate what the child knows, and what the child actually needs to know. When you've been at your home education program for a year, whether or not the child is in school, it's time to take a brief look at how far you've come and how far you have to go before you can relax in the knowledge that your child has been failure-proofed by a mastery of the basics.

SIX

The Second Year

You've been home teaching a year now. Let's say you started your formal home supplement program when your child was five years old, and the child is now six. Where should you be in terms of what the child knows?

If you followed the instructions and started the child out on "Sesame Street" when he or she was three or four, and started a daily exploration of the alphabet and words at five, the child should be reading now. That's encouraging right there, because some public school students never learn to read at all, and in all but the very best schools they could still be struggling with the alphabet at this age.

If you have any doubts about where your child stands in terms of reading, you can set up an informal test. You may want to make a little party out of it, with a cupcake topped with a candle and a funny hat. Children love this sort of thing, and it's heartwarming for the parents too. It also helps augment all the school plays and pageants that the public schools use to appeal to doting parents and grandparents. These shows are fun, but be wary. It doesn't matter how cute Bobby and Jennifer look when they're dressed up as a teapot and a sunflower. If they are not learning to read, *cute* will wear off awfully fast.

After you've had your miniparty to celebrate the child's first year of home schooling, take the child to his or her lesson for the day. Piled on a table will be a stack of books the child has never seen before. These books range from simple books with one sentence on each page to more difficult books where the whole page is large-print text. The child should be encouraged to read a few pages from each book aloud to see how well he or she pronounces. From time to time, you should stop the child and ask if he or she liked the story, and what he or she liked or didn't like about it. This is elementary good manners, which should be at least as important between parent and child as between total strangers. It's also a good way to judge the child's comprehension.

A rule of thumb is when the child stumbles over more than five words on a given page or large paragraph, he or she has gone over his or her head. This is the child's reading level. If you can find some school readers — children's libraries may have them in the stacks — you can judge what level your child has reached in public school terms.

There is no way, at the age of six, that your child is a problem reader yet. But if he or she has not progressed well in reading, you may want to give special attention to the next chapter, in which a love of reading and good reading habits are encouraged.

The math evaluation of the first year's progress can be simply done. Bounce about 10 or 12 questions from addition or subtraction off the child and see if he or she knows the times tables thoroughly. If the child does know it all, well and good. If not, this is the place to concentrate your efforts for another full year, if need be. More students foul up in advanced math through a lack of knowledge of the times tables and the elementary skills than for any other reason.

If the student is not doing well in math, you have plenty of time to play catch-up. But don't fail to do so. You may want to make the math lessons shorter, but do them twice a day, so the child actually spends more time on his or her times tables but doesn't get as bored with them. Remember that the goal is not to produce a child prodigy—it's to make sure that the basic skills are in good order.

If the student is doing well in math, solid in the times tables and in addition and subtraction, it may be time to start more advanced math.

One of the things you will want to work on is division. You begin this level with the good old counting frame. It is as simple as multiplication in reverse, which is why it is so absolutely vital to know the times tables perfectly before starting.

Set up all 10 beads of the first row on the counting frame. Ask the child: "How many sets of two are there in 10?" Let him or her count them. Then do the old matha-magic game a few times and show the child that you can call off the number of sets faster, by dividing in your head, than he or she can by counting the beads. Your ability will fill the child with curiosity about how to do this.

The next step is to write out the division table for all the even multiples of 2: 2, 4, 6, 8, 10, 12, 14, 16, 18, and so on. Put them in division boxes and let the child write in the correct answers. And make sure that he or she writes only the correct answers, because mistakes at this age are hard to overcome. Learning early has to be learned correctly if it's going to be worth anything.

From here, you add a line at a time until the child can divide all the even multiples of 2, 3, 4, 5, 6, 7, 8, and 9. It's important to ground the child just as thoroughly in division as it is in multiplication. One of the benefits of starting division early—and one-on-one—is that children are more patient than most adults realize when they aren't distracted by TV sets or other children. They should master these basics early so they can have a firm footing when they move on to more complicated forms of math. Another reason to stress rote is that younger children don't handle abstraction well. It's a serious mistake—and the source of much needless parent-child friction between gifted parents and gifted children—to try to force even the most basic algebra or geometry on a bright child before the child is eight or nine. Even if the child has mastered the times tables at five, he or she will not be ready for the kind of logic that higher mathematics requires. Tests across all lines of IQ and culture substantiate this tendency of smaller children, however bright, to be deficient in abstract reasoning capacity.

Once you understand their limitation, your best bet is to keep reinforcing your early lead in arithmetic. You can, if you want, teach the child how to add by *carrying* numbers or to subtract by *borrowing*. But if you let them carry or borrow, make sure you let them write the number being carried or borrowed in the space above the problem until they learn to carry or borrow with complete confidence.

Another math concept you can begin to explain, because it's concrete, is fractions. One of the best ways to do fractions is to find some pieces of paper that are completely square — or cut some. Fold one sheet in half. Explain to the child what one half means and then write ½ on each side of the paper. Next, fold a second sheet into quarters by folding it in half vertically, then horizontally. Explain what one ¼ means and write ¼ on each folded section of the paper.

If the child demonstrates mathematical skills after having mastered the basics, you can buy supplemental instruction books in math and move the child along at his or her own speed. Some children will master math skills up to the sixth grade level in their second or third year of school. Boys excel more often than girls do, but don't ever tell your daughter "girls aren't good at math," any more than you would tell your son that "boys don't like to read." The child may get so involved in trying to live up to his or her gender identity that the child will sacrifice a genuine ability in the interests of conformity.

If the child doesn't show great affinity for math but has a solid competence, don't push him or her much beyond the child's grade level. The purpose of supplemental home education is to cover the gaps in the child's regular school education, not to produce an annoying precocious prodigy whom the other kids and the teachers come to detest. Some schools do an adequate job of math basics, and in these schools you may be satisfied if the child is getting straight A's and knows as much as he or she should at the proper age and grade level. But a warning buzzer should go off in your head if the child hasn't started the times table by the second grade and completely absorbed it by the third grade. You should keep this area under direct control through home teaching, whatever the child is doing in school, and however satisfied the teachers profess to be.

One of the best supplements Emily and Johnny discovered, once they had mastered the basics of math was "Square One," a PBS math show aired after school hours during the school months of the year. Some of the rock music, rock dancing, and rock-'em-sock-'em dramatics of this show may offend more conservative parents, but it's a great incentive to turn on a show in which the kids learn about *palindromes* and *combinatorics* — without being tied to their chairs.

"Square One" is often paired with "Three-Two-One Contact," an introductory science show geared to preadolescents in junior high school and fifth and sixth grades. There is no reason at all why a bright home schooler should not watch both of these shows each day, even though the episodes are sometimes repeated three or four times a season.

"Three-Two-One-Contact" includes science tours of Greece, Malaysia, France, England, Japan, and various parts of the United States. The show revolves around weekly series of five episodes each, which either deal with a specific country or a specific topic. One week the theme may be *models*, the next week *mammals*, and the following week an exploration of a buried city on the Island of Crete, with a discussion of modern and ancient Greek culture. The show could be criticized slightly because it almost completely neglects to use mathematics in science, but in terms of arousing interest and offering basic facts, it's a winner.

A concerned parent, aware of the damage that too much television inflicts on study time, may be wary of suggesting that the child watch an extra hour of TV each day. The easy solution is to promote "Square One" and "Three-Two-One Contact" as a privilege, even a reward, rather than an assignment. These shows really *are* entertaining enough that most children will watch them voluntarily—but make sure that they don't switch to cartoons when your back is turned. An hour of "Three-Two-One Contact" and "Square One" is an absolutely different proposition than an hour of "Ghost Busters" and "Teenage Mutant Ninja Turtles."

Your first year of teaching a foreign language may not be the same as the first year of home education. Many parents will prefer to wait until the child has mastered basic reading and the times tables before introducing a new subject as potentially challenging as French or German.

The first-year review of your child's prowess in foreign languages should wait until he or she has been studying the specific language for a year, or possibly as much as 18 months. This means that—if the language selected is French—the child will have finished two passes through both *See It and Say It in French* and *Fun with French,* and will be well acquainted with *Mon Premier Dictionnaire.* You can judge how well the child is actually learning by having him or her read a story from the end of *Fun with French* or *See It and Say It,* which contain a few full pages of simple text toward the end of the books. Ask the child to explain the text word for word. If the child seems to be decoding the French properly, you have done your job well.

Now it's time for further evaluation—and some fun. Take the child on a jaunt to a library, sit him or her down in a quiet corner, and stack up all the available children's picture books in the language the child has been studying. You'll probably find them all together under 448 in the Dewey Decimal Code. Shuffle the books from the easiest to the hardest, and find out if the child can read and translate books he or she has not seen before. If the child does well, the child's happiness should be palpable—and make sure you praise him or her effusively.

Now may be the time for a serious decision. If your child has a solid footing in one language, and seems to show an affinity to foreign languages, it may be time to start a second language.

In *The Principles of Psychology*, William James said if a child is going to learn a foreign language without an accent, and with a maximum of retention and a minimum of stress, the child should start the specific language before the age of 10. In this sense, only, is there a bit of a rush. Some colleges require only one foreign language, many require none, but I know people in advanced academic programs who deeply regret that they didn't start German when their minds were still flexible and highly retentive. The same is true if you intend to teach the child any language that is not written with the Roman (English) alphabet. Job opportunities reach out to the native-born American who is politically reliable and speaks Russian, Chinese, Japanese, or Arabic. I recommend these choices only to the child who is linguistically oriented. But if the child *can* master a language not written with the Roman alphabet, some authorities claim this ability will not only expand their job horizons but their functional IQs.

There is a wonderful book available in most larger children's libraries called *You Can Write Chinese*, by Kurt Wiese, which tells the story of how an American boy learns the simplest Chinese characters. I don't seriously recommend a full course in the Chinese-Japanese system of ideographs for the average home schooler. In most cases it's better to stick to the standard languages, like French, Spanish, or German. But a brief introduction to the Chinese-Japanese system of writing through *You Can Write Chinese* is a superb mindstretcher. Old-fashioned racist psychologists used to argue that the Chinese and Japanese turned their children's brains to gray mush by forcing them to learn the 1,800 basic characters and 4,000-plus combinations needed to understand Chinese-Japanese classics. Today, given the awesome superiority of Japanese and Chinese students to American kids in mathematics and that Asians usually score higher than either whites or blacks on cross-cultural IQ tests, some authorities wonder if the difficult picture-writing system might not stimulate intellectual growth. In any case, the ability to read just a handful of Chinese characters is a major confidence builder to children and a good introduction to the world's largest nation—China—and to an economic superpower—Japan.

I particularly remember one brutally hot summer a few years ago, when Emily was 10 and Johnny was 6. We endured 31 back-to-back days of 90-plus degree weather, and during the afternoons when I was home the kids and I curtailed lessons and adjourned to the backyard swimming pool. The pool was a prefab, 18 inches deep, and about 8 feet across, so nobody learned to swim. While we lolled in the water, we studied *You Can Read Chinese* in the shade and wrote the characters on sheets of paper we had put up so we could see them from the pool. We beat the heat until evening came when we could resume lessons inside the house.

The water was too shallow to learn to swim, and the lessons were too shallow to say the children actually learned the Chinese system of writing. But just as they lost their fear of the water, they lost their fear of reading Chinese.

Later both children learned to swim in a bigger pool. If they ever need to learn Chinese—or anything else equally exotic and difficult—the self-confidence and the basic understanding they picked up that broiling summer will stand them in good stead.

By the end of the first year, the child should have lost any fear of the learning process. One of the worst services mass education does to slower students is to convince them that they are somehow flawed as people because they're slower learners than their classmates. The edge of self-confidence, once lost, is seldom recovered. The home-supplementing parent should also have gauged the capacity of the student. Rather than pushing the student too fast, the home teacher should have learned to adjust the lessons to the student's own best pace.

Teaching a Love of Reading

Have you ever told your son or daughter to "go read something"?

I'll bet I can guess what happened. A short time after you told them and the child walked away, you found him or her watching TV, staring out the window, or running around in circles imitating a car or a cement mixer.

Reading is essential. But it's not as natural as breathing, eating, drinking, or sleeping—or playing. Some children—most of them female—take off as soon as they begin decoding and read everything that comes their way. Some other children—mostly boys—have to be browbeaten into reading anything more verbose than a road sign.

We have the authority of the public schools, and of the U.S. government, that reading is a desirable activity. All sorts of programs exist to encourage reading. You've seen the commercials on TV, which in itself may be part of the problem. Probably neither you nor the child were reading when you saw the commercial. My son saw one of them. He was mortified.

"Look! A kid *that* age reading a *baby book* like *that!* Wow! I guess they got to him too late, huh, Dad?"

Let me point out Johnny was not born literate. Let me also

point out, at the age of nine, he had still been known to stare out the window, imitate a car or a cement mixer, and switch on cartoons on TV when he was the first one up on Saturday morning. But he does read books, regularly and often voluntarily. And his sister gobbles down books several years above her age-level the way some kids munch out on junk food.

It can be done. Here's how to do it.

The first thing you have to remember about reading is that it's a first-rate tool of education, but a third-rate approach to reality. There's absolutely nothing any school system can do for a kid who can't or won't read. If he or she is there, the child is taking up space and wasting time. On the other hand, books are not real life. Real life is real life. TV, movies, and recorded music are a secondary approach to real life. Reading is a third hand approach. The mind not only has to perceive, but to decode or decipher a book to get a glimpse of reality. This ability is tough enough for a child to do when he or she is just learning to read. When the child has to compete with TV, squabbling siblings, or constant interruptions for chores or questions about matters not related to what he or she is reading, it may be impossible. And one of the reasons Americans are comparatively poor readers is because our on-the-go lifestyle doesn't give children the time or concentration they need for serious reading.

I love classical music. At home I listen to symphonies, operas, concertos and rhapsodies for hours at a time, sometimes when I'm writing and other times when I'm relaxing. But I can't stand to listen to classical music when I'm out running errands in the car, doing stop-to-stop driving and getting in and out of the car at five-minute intervals. Classical music doesn't fit in with five-minute, start-and-stop driving. If your house is in constant turmoil—as many houses are—the household doesn't really fit the reading situation.

The first lesson, then, is to allow the child who is just learning to read some time during the day when he or she won't be disturbed or distracted. Set aside an hour a day—not time you have to be directly supervising the child, because that would add too many hours to any supplemental-teaching schedule. The child, not you, should set this time aside from his or her schedule. Tell yourself, over and over, that during this time the child will *not* be told to pick up his or her socks, water the plants, or vacuum the living room. Nor will the child be allowed to come to the telephone when friends call or go outside and play. This time is reading time. Period.

Parental respect for reading is important. In Asian countries, children in school sometimes place the book about to be read on their school desks and bow their heads to it, to show respect for the author. I think that's a little extreme. But if parents don't show respect for reading, by reading themselves and allowing their children the time and concentration needed to read, they're not going to produce good readers except by accident.

When the child has his or her reading time, the child should be prepared. If there's eating to be done, do it before the reading time starts. The same holds for trips to the bathroom. Smaller children, who are just learning to read, may be allowed to cuddle a stuffed animal if they want to—but not action toys. Above all, the child's reading area should be in an area where he or she can't see or hear the TV.

Popular music tends to interrupt concentration. Rock and jazz music tend to shatter it. Hearing classical music, especially if it's entirely orchestral, or if the singing is in a foreign language the child doesn't understand, may actually help foster concentration by screening out street or household noises. Try it and see if you get better results with classical music or just with silence. But above all—no rock music and no TV.

Now that you have the child's reading area organized, what do they read?

Just for a few moments, imagine that you're six, seven, or eight years old. Somebody stuffs a book in your hands and tells you to read it. What's your reaction? Confusion? Resentment? Fear? If it's any of these things, you probably won't enjoy the book much. And if it happens all the time, you'll probably never develop a love of reading.

The first lesson of this imaginary voyage back in time is to offer the child those books that you would like if you were a child. The ideal starter books will be beautifully illustrated, have plenty of pictures, large print, and interesting stories. You can't go wrong with the books that children have always loved more than all others—*Aesop's Fables, Grimm's Fairy Tales,* and the tales of Charles Perrault.

Those three books have interesting backgrounds. Aesop is said to have been a crippled Phrygian slave, who lived about a hundred years before the great age of Greece. He made his living telling stories that had morals. These stories are some of the greatest mind openers of all times. No child should be without them. After I received a copy myself when I was a slow reader in second grade, I took the book on a one-week vacation and read the stories until I had virtually memorized them. When I returned from my vacation, my whole attitude toward reading had changed, and my reading level in the next school year shot up from below my grade level to junior high school level while I was a third-grader.

Happily, the version of *Aesop's Fables* I enjoyed so much is still available. This fine book, with the same artwork, is published by Illustrated Junior Library, a subsidiary of Grosset and Dunlap. Many timeless childhood classics are available in the same series. I recommend *Aesop's Fables* as an absolute requirement of any home schooling program.

Grimm's Fairy Tales is also available in the traditional English-language version through the Illustrated Junior Library. I recommend this book as second only to Aesop. The original book, in German, was called *Kinder und Hausmärchen* (Children and House Tales). Jacob and Wilhelm Grimm collected the stories and wrote them down in the original dialects in the years just after the Napoleonic Wars when mandatory public schooling first spread through the German states, partly because they wanted to collect stories, but mostly because they wanted to preserve the dialects that they realized would disappear once most Germans became literate. The book became a surprise bestseller among educated people who wanted to read the stories to their children. The book's appeal has lasted almost 200 years.

Charles Perrault, the third great storyteller, recorded such classics as "Puss in Boots," "Bluebeard," and "Cinderella" in a book he wrote, under his son's name, to help the boy court royal favor. These stories are also vital and fascinating. While children might have already seen them in cartoons, with or without your supervision, they will be interested in the original translated version.

The classic children's tales have been criticized for a lack of *relevance* because they are set in far-off times and far-off places. But they offer all the important features of any great story—excitement, suspense, clear-cut characterization. And children really do love them.

If your child is truly an enthusiastic reader, you can offer one or more of these books as a birthday or holiday present. If the child is a reluctant reader, the *gift* approach is still a good idea. But you may want to sit side by side with the child and read through the book, one story at a time. The child will probably want to read these stories again and again. Adults, raised in a word of disposable fiction, detective stories, and thrillers, may wonder if it's entirely normal for a child to reread these stories. Don't worry! The child is developing his or her own self-confidence, besides visiting old friends. If the child wants to read the same book three or four times, there's no harm in it, especially if it's a classic or a work of history.

One of the ways to reinforce a child's interest in reading is to make the subject visual. If you have the chance, it's sometimes a good idea to introduce a child to the world of folk tales and fairy tales with one or more of the Disney feature-length cartoons. These cartoons are available through VCR tape rentals, if you don't encounter them on a regular broadcast schedule. Viewing these cartoons overcomes a serious problem. When the child first opens a book and sees a mass of little black words on white paper, it doesn't look anything like a story about people. The pictures help overcome this blot-out effect. A film version will overcome it even more. The child will go over the story's text with a sense of familiarity that encourages interest and self-confidence.

Once the child learns that reading can be fun, the battle is half over. At this point, instead of spoon-feeding the child through side-by-side reading, the home schooling parent can move the child toward self-sufficiency through independent reading.

The parent now has to shift from being a "motivator" — in other words, a bookpusher — to being an observer. Find out what the child really wants to read, and if the subject isn't harmful, just stoke the blaze as literacy flares up.

Emily's early reading years benefited because of a particular incident: one of my wife's lady friends, Barbara Harrington, gave my wife some things her own daughter had outgrown. Among the toys Emily found was an old, somewhat battered copy of *The Bobbsey Twins at the Seashore*. At this point Emily could read, but still needed some prodding to pick up a book on her own. She turned the Bobbsey Twins book over curiously and paged through it.

I asked her, a day or two later, if she had enjoyed it.

"Yeah, it was really good! There are these two sets of twins, Bert and Nan and Freddy and Flossie, and they help their father solve mysteries . . . Freddy and Flossie are just six, but they're pretty smart."

I had seen a whole stack of Bobbsey Twins books in a store downtown, so the next day I bought one and gave it to Emily.

"This is a reward for a job well done," I said, after her math lesson was over. "Keep up the good work and there'll be more where this came from."

She read it in two days and wanted another one.

For the next six months, I bought Bobbsey Twins books on a regular basis, two or three a week. Emily seemed to read them faster than I could buy them. One day she read two of them, back to back, within a time span of three or four hours.

Her peers in school were still puzzling over *cat, rat,* and *hat.*

I know, as a professional writer, that these books are turned out by formula and that the author is probably six different people. But the books themselves, while not designed to appeal to adult critics, are not just harmless. They're extremely constructive. The mysteries are nonviolent, and they take place at locations around the nation and the globe. The child learns something about Japan, or Greece, or Hawaii as well as sharpening reading skills that can go blunt with too much television. I'm very glad that Barbara Harrington gave us that first Bobbsey Twins book. The series helped turn Emily from an average reader into an avid reader.

Emily later moved to Nancy Drew stories and consumed them almost as greedily as she had eaten up Bobbsey Twins books. I didn't mind buying her copies at the store downtown, because pride of ownership and the joy of receiving presents plays a big role in the encouragement of reading. But, if money or convenience prevents regular purchases, books in both series are available in the children's sections of most libraries.

One of my wife's favorite books as a child was *Anne of Green Gables.* She used to talk about the book all the time. I myself would not have been caught dead reading a girl's book like that when I was an adolescent. My taste went straight from children's storybooks and comics to war stories and tales of explorers and the sea, with a later digression into Shakespeare, and finally to French and German classics in their original languages. I didn't have any idea what *Anne of Green Gables* was about or what it was like, so I was in no position to join my wife in advocating that Emily read her mother's favorite childhood classic.

I bought Emily a copy of the book and she paged through the introduction but couldn't push herself any further. I didn't put the screws on and force her. It's always a mistake to ram something down a kid's throat. The kid will invariably hate the book, and may even come to dislike reading in general.

So the Illustrated Junior Library version of *Anne of Green Gables* gathered dust on the bookshelf for about 18 months after I had bought it.

In February of 1986, I read in *TV GUIDE* that *Anne of Green Gables* was about to be telecast in a new version on PBS. I decided to make a VCR tape recording as a gift to my wife, knowing how much she had loved the story since childhood. The film was billed as "heartwarming" and even as "sweet." It was heartwarming and sweet but what exploded on the TV screen was the adolescent genius of the two juvenile stars, Megan Follows as "Anne," and Schuyler Grant as "Diana," as well as stellar performances by a superb supporting cast. Greatness flashed out of almost every scene, and the cinematography by Rene Ohashi was gorgeous, like an Impressionist painting come to life. Kevin Sullivan's version of *Anne of Green Gables* was probably the best children's movie of the 1980s—and I wasn't the only one who thought so. Emily took the dusty book down from the shelf and read it from cover to cover in two days. She asked for more books about Anne. She went through the entire series by Lucy Maud Montgomery, and later took up the Emily series by Lucy Maud Montgomery as well, reading all of them. True enough, *Anne of Green Gables* showed signs of becoming a full-time obsession. I realized this when Emily formed the habit of climbing atop an iron lawn chair to declaim poetry, as Megan Follows did in *Anne.* But who would you rather have your preteenage daughter imitate—Megan Follows, playing Anne Shirley, the virginal "Little Miss Bookworm," or Madonna, singing smut in her underwear?

Emily shortly announced that she was the president of "The Anne Club," which was dedicated to advancing and publicizing *Anne of Green Gables* and to advocating a sequel. When a sequel was shortly authorized, starring most of the same people, she was elated. At this point, she had written a number of fan letters to Megan Follows and Schuyler Grant and received replies. Her dedication to the film had not only encouraged good reading habits, but opened up a whole world in which celebrities were real people and a movie was something that was created, not something that happened when you flicked on the TV set.

Anne of Green Gables put the final seal of acceptance on full-time recreational reading as far as Emily was concerned. Johnny was a different case. He had an easier time learning math than his sister, and was generally more aggressive and not as shy. But if Emily had a mild case of reading resistance, Johnny was a case study.

"Johnny, sit down and read something!"

He would plunk in a chair. Pick up a book. But five minutes later, he would be doing something else—anything else. Johnny was probably the only kid I had ever encountered who considered cleaning his room a desirable alternative to reading. Ask him to shovel snow or wash the car, and he would beam with pride when he showed you a job well done without any supervision. Take your eyes off him when he had been set down with a book and he would be gone, or sleeping, within a matter of minutes.

But not anymore.

One of the things Johnny liked was "Davy Crockett." I once rented a VCR tape to show my children the kind of TV shows I had enjoyed as a kid, and they both enjoyed it immensely. A few months later, the whole Walt Disney "Davy Crockett" series with Fess Parker and Buddy Ebsen was shown in the proper sequential order, and we taped them all. Johnny might not sit down and read without being bound or shackled, but he had no trouble sitting through two or three "Davy Crockett" episodes back to back.

So we made a deal. I checked out some library books about Davy Crockett. He was allowed to watch an episode every time he finished two chapters of a book. In this way, he could make his way through a book in two or three days, without being coerced or threatened.

At one point, he sat down to read his two chapters of a Davy Crockett book before he was allowed to turn on his tape. I was on my way to work, so I left him sitting on the living room sofa with the book. I assumed he just might jump up and switch on Fess Parker as soon as my back was turned. But I also knew there was a streak of stubborn honesty in Johnny that tended to make him keep his word.

A few minutes into the drive, I remembered that I had left my camera at home and that I needed it at work. I turned around to return home. On the way back I was caught in some mild traffic and didn't arrive home for about 30 minutes. I entered the house quietly. Johnny was still sitting on the sofa reading the book. He looked surprised to see me.

"You're still reading two chapters?" I asked.

Johnny puzzled over the book for a moment as he paged through it.

"Hey! I read six chapters! I forgot I was reading!"

I sensed victory.

Johnny needed motivation, but he now read fluently. One day I learned that Dorothy Gramatky and Linda Gramatky Smith, the wife and daughter of Hardie Gramatky, creator of *Little Toot,* were holding an autograph session in a bookstore a few miles from our home to celebrate the release of *Little Toot and the Loch Ness Monster.* I had loved Little Toot as a child, and I made a point of taking Johnny to the autograph session with me. The two ladies were friendly and charming, and besides acquiring autographed copies of the book, I took Johnny's picture with them.

A few weeks later, his favorite computer at the library was out of order. Without any suggestion from me, Johnny read every Little Toot book in the library while he was waiting for the computer to be fixed. "They're my friends," he explained, when somebody asked why he wanted to read every Little Toot book in the library.

When people are insecure, they seek out the familiar and the friendly. Young readers are often insecure about reading. They tend to seek the familiar—characters, styles, and even stories that they already know. There's nothing wrong with this. The child who sets out to read every book in a series should be encouraged at all costs. Reading is one thing you get better at only through constant practice. Above all, keep your child reading anything for the first two or three years after he or she learns to decode in one-on-one lessons with you or with a regular teacher.

One of the best ways to encourage active reading is to let the child subscribe to his or her own magazine. There's something about waiting for the postal carrier, finding the magazine in the mailbox, and taking it back into the house with a feeling of discovery that promotes an eagerness to read. Our two family favorites were *Cricket* and *Highlights for Children.* (I confess a conflict of interest in that both of them have published stories I wrote for them after I began to explore the world of childhood by teaching at home.) When she was 4 years old, Emily started out with *Highlights* shortly after she learned to decode independently. She also picked up on *Cricket.* By the time she was seven, she was still reading *Highlights* and *Cricket* but had also moved on to *Reader's Digest.* By the time she was 11, she had her own subscription to *Time,* which she had been able to read with understanding several years earlier.

Boys being boys, Johnny started out a bit slower. He wasn't really decoding until he was almost 5, but by 6 he was reading *Cricket* and *Highlights* every time they arrived. When he was 8, he moved on to *Reader's Digest,* and before he was 10 he surprised us all by taking out a pay-as-you-go subscription to *Newsweek* — probably because his sister was reading *Time.*

It goes without saying that reading is the single most important aspect of education. What many parents don't understand is the joy of having literate, civilized, and well-informed children — and the immense feeling of satisfaction at having helped them get that way, either by yourselves or with the help of the school systems.

EIGHT

TV—Friend or Foe? Or Both?

The abuse of TV has probably been the single greatest factor in declining test scores, the strange phenomenon of the middle-class 12-year-old who can barely read, and the cultural illiteracy of a startling number of college freshmen—and college graduates.

Some pollsters have calculated that by the time the average American child is 16 years old, he or she will have witnessed 200,000 violent episodes on the screen. This fact may explain the lack of concern many people show when they ignore someone being murdered or maimed in a public place.

Some of my younger friends blame soap operas, the staple of daytime TV, for the breakup of their marriages. They claim their young wives see so many rich, handsome, sexy men on daytime TV that they just can't adjust to the reality of a hardworking husband who comes home exhausted after working a full-time job, plus a part-time job, just to make ends meet. So the wife walks out.

Some wives also blame TV for failed or *dead* marriages. They claim their husbands get so involved in spectator sports that they never talk.

Television, in either of these contexts, and in the terrible amount of time that's taken away from children's and teenagers' reading and study time, is a blight on the landscape. But there's another side to the story. TV is one of the best tools available for opening up new subjects to children who are just learning to read or preparing to explore new eras in history or fields in science and geography.

The important point to remember is that TV itself is not a monster. It's the misuse of TV that turns the tube into such a negative force.

We've already gone over the use of TV in a strictly educational context to help teach reading and to enrich the teaching of foreign languages. These uses of TV are a vital part of the program. This chapter will suggest some ways in which the bug-eyed monster can be tamed, even when it can't be harnessed to the home schooling program.

Television programs should be divided into three categories: those that are constructive and educational; those that are neutral and harmless even if they're academically worthless; and those that are forbidden.

The forbidden category isn't too hard to define. Among my favorite candidates for the Hall of Dishonor would be anything pornographic or pointlessly violent. Few parents, especially those interested in a Christian approach to home schooling, would disagree with this standard as a definition of bad or even forbidden entertainment. But do they always know how widely this definition can be applied?

I remember once picking Emily up at her sewing lessons. She had become so good at sewing that the teacher invited her back as an assistant instructor. She was 11 years old and quite proud of this honor, and she took her job very seriously.

Emily was bustling around, helping the teacher straighten up the shop. While she was working, the other students clustered around the drafty front door, waiting for their mothers to nudge their cars through the gathering traffic and rescue them from boredom. Two of the girls were teaching the others a song. I picked up on some of the words: "They say she's mean but I don't care, I love makin' love to her wild, wild hair . . ."

The name of this song, I was told, was "I Want Your Sex." The girls who were cavorting around singing were six and seven years old.

The use of the TV for rock videos—dirty songs and dirty dancing, often with perverse, antireligious, or satanic themes, and almost always with truly awful music—is one of the worst uses of TV in any context. Making this kind of programming available to preteenagers, in my opinion, defies description in its mental and moral idiocy. If you try to suggest this point to certain mothers, they will reply with righteous indignation:

"Everybody does it!"

That's one of the reasons why I don't trust peer groups as the source for values. The sort of people who use "everybody does it" as an excuse for their own moral cowardice and appalling bad taste obviously can't form sensible opinions of their own, or exert a wholesome influence on their own children. I don't want them exerting a secondhand influence on mine. The kid who grows up listening to Mozart or Beethoven will have no trouble recognizing that Heavy Metal is junkyard music—with or without its satanic overtones. Fans of Joan Sutherland, Luciano Pavarotti, and Placido Domingo laugh up their sleeves at the parody of music that's foisted on kids by peer pressure. Some of the rock musicians of the 1960s actually had voices. Most of the "talents" around today can't sing their way out of an airline barf-bag. Their "handlers" keep their careers alive by promoting the fact that parents hate the music—and that kids can rebel by loving it.

The problem, of course, is mass popular ignorance of what constitutes genuine music. Most of the real brains behind the rock industry, like the composers of "Tin Pan Alley" two generations before, learned their trade listening to classical composers. The single greatest influence behind rock music once it broke from its original roots among southern black performers was probably—are your ready for this?—Richard Wagner, the ultimate composer of *heavy* opera. Patriotic Americans were trained to upchuck when Wagner's name was mentioned a generation ago, because his posthumous admirers included Adolf Hitler and the Nazis. But Phil Spector's "wall-of-sound" technique, which created the rock music of the 1960s, was an acknowledged knockoff of Wagner's orchestration.

Since TV plays such a vital role in promoting bad music, you can turn the tables by letting the children listen to real music. Many of Wagner's operas are available on VCR tapes. So are the mellower operas of Mozart, Rossini, and Verdi. Wagner, however, has one advantage over the other composers when dealing with kids whose tastes have been warped by "Heavy Metal"—his consummate barbarism. Kids listen to rock music to defy adults. The music itself is usually terrible. Wagner's music is also widely hated because he had a crabby personality, chased women frantically, wrote bad checks and vicious slurs against his rivals—especially those rivals who were Jewish—and generally behaved like a bigot and a scoundrel. There is one crucial difference between Richard Wagner and the average rock composer. Wagner was a genius when he wrote music. His operas revolve around murder, rape, adultery, and crimes of greed and lust, but unlike the MTV version, these deeds are recognized as evil and destructive, not as healthy forms of recreation.

The four-part *Ring of the Nibelungs,* 20 hours of blood and thunder, contains just about every known crime—and every punishment as well. After Wagner wore himself out with the *Ring,* he made a celebrated and sincere conversion back to Christianity and wrote *Parsifal,* one of the most Christian of all great stage works. Wagner's detractors are legion. His admirers, almost without exception, however, include the upper 2 or 3 percent of the population in intellect and income. Outside the English-speaking world, his works have the same cachet that Shakespeare has to people who read English. Introducing a bright child to Wagner and to Verdi, the greatest nineteenth-century Italian composer, whose music is more accessible though less intellectual, will form a permanent sound barrier between the child and Heavy Metal.

Most children, however, don't watch a lot of opera. They watch a lot of cartoons. This seems harmless enough, and it *is* harmless when they watch Walt Disney cartoons. Some of Disney's feature-length cartoons are genuine works of art, and none are corrupting influences. This is not true of every cartoon that flickers across the TV screen on Saturday morning. Most of the mass-produced, poorly animated cartoons that are shown when adults are apt to be catching up on their sleep are concocted not so much to entertain children as to convince them to beg for the toys created as spin-offs for the cartoons. There's a name for this Saturday morning cartoon festival. It's called "Kid-Vid." Unthinking adults may be delighted to see the kids staring at cartoons instead of horror movies or semipornographic MTV videos of rock singers orchestrating blasphemies and incitements to rape. It's absolutely true that cartoons aren't as damaging as slasher films of guts and gore. But too many parents don't stop to think that if the kids weren't immersed in crassly commercial cartoons, they might be watching something educational or even be reading.

The worst aspect of some cartoons is that they teach children that violence doesn't really hurt. The funny cat in the cartoons gets run over by a steamroller. He's squashed as flat as a pancake. He reinflates by blowing air into his thumb, gets up, and walks away—unhurt. People get blown 50 feet into the air and land smoldering and smoking. A few moments later, they're back to normal. This visual action may be funny if you're an adult. If you're a small child, however, the message is you can get run over or blown up and walk away laughing. That's the extreme case. The more common lesson is that the appropriate response to any frustrating situation is to punch somebody. Kids rampage at school hitting each other, and hitting smaller children, and sometimes even teachers, because they spend hours every day watching cartoons where the "good guys" and the "bad guys" alike run around punching heads. The child who has been raised by human beings and not by TV enters a schoolroom filled with "TV children" at a physical disadvantage. The "people child" has usually been taught that violence is wrong, or at very least that it's the last resort of self-defense. The "TV child" has been taught by his surrogate parent—the TV set— that violence is fun. It's neat. It's cool. Everybody does it. And the teacher runs around trying to stop fights every 30 seconds.

Beyond the kiddie cartoons with their cast of hyperactive animals, there are war and space cartoons featuring more sophisticated forms of violence. These too are marketed in tandem with all kinds of toys. The values they teach are more subtly corrosive. In recent years, the "good guys" are a sort of All-American Platoon featuring Afro-Americans and women along with the usual cast of Aryan supermales. The "villains" are often subhuman creatures bent on world domination. The message, of course, is that violence in resisting evil is no crime. The facts of life, however, are that wars don't take place between clean-cut kids from Cincinnati and humanoid reptiles. Real wars take place between rival groups of humans. The idea that a "war picture" is a cartoon doesn't make it any less disturbing. In fact, by inserting the ultimate dehumanization of the enemy, who turns up as a reptile or a walking skeleton, the cartoon becomes the ultimate in proviolent propaganda. I would much rather let my children watch the old black-and-white version of *All Quiet on the Western Front,* in which nice guys die screaming with pain and fear, and in which the scared young German who stabs a scared middle-aged Frenchman is tormented by guilt and shame as he watches his victim die. *All Quiet on the Western Front* provides a view of what war between two civilized powers is actually like.

The child, of course, will come away stunned and horrified after seeing a gruesome depiction of dozens of violent and painful deaths. Wars, however, aren't waged as a form of entertainment. And for that reason I think viewing war cartoons, containing models of military machines that have never actually existed, is a mistake. The idea that the slain enemy isn't human is probably the worst part of all. It's an idea that tyrants and fanatics have traded on throughout history, most notably in the Hitler-Stalin era. And it's an idea that we can all do without, even if we aren't strict pacifists.

Films that promote promiscuity, bisexuality, or pointless violence are obviously on my personal dump list. What's on the list for *neutral* or *harmless?* For openers, I would nominate anything that's not smutty or gory, but also does not inspire, inform, or educate. This broad stroke covers most of what's on prime-time TV, other than the news and documentaries. Lonely people, or those who have boring and troubled family lives, often get roped into following the lives of TV families as if they were watching real people. Supermarket tabloids cater to the fantasies that TV families are real, and relevant. The cover stories feature all sorts of crisis stories about the members of the TV families.

In a world where so many people live states or continents away from their own extended families, those substitute families may serve some sort of psychological need for lonely adults. But what purpose do they serve for children? The child usually has a mother and father, possibly brothers and sisters. The child already *has* a family. He or she doesn't need a substitute family, or five or six substitute families, on the tube once a week. Most situation comedies are "popcorn entertainment." They don't cause cancer or cavities, but they don't provide much nutrition either. When there is a choice, it's better to turn the TV off and let the child read. If the child is read out and feels that he or she has to watch something on TV, you can provide a show that's educational or at least better entertainment by means of the VCR. But the best idea is still reading. The more the child does it, the more the child likes it.

If some TV is forbidden, and if other shows are permitted but not encouraged, what's worth watching on TV other than programs with classical music?

For openers, of course, there's a regular battery of educational programs available on PBS or on some of the cable channels if you have cable. You can find everything from shows that teach reading, as we've already discussed, to shows on physics, biology, and home economics. Some of these shows may be far beyond the level of the child you're teaching. But you will find that when children don't have to face repeated testing, they can absorb a considerable amount of information—more than you might imagine.

One day Emily and Johnny had gone out with me on a half-day assignment. I was to take pictures of a Fourth of July parade for a newspaper, and I thought the children might enjoy the costumes, the floats, the vintage and antique cars, and the bands. We arrived about 45 minutes early because I had to make sure to find a parking space in Denville, New Jersey, a town noted for its parking problems, though it's a likable town in many other ways. The heat was about 90°, and there was no shade. While we were waiting for the parade to form, we ran into Lorenzo Cassetta, the old Italian-American gentleman who lived in an apartment overlooking the line-of-march and knew me by sight. Cassetta saw the children tagging along and asked if they would like to come inside and enjoy the shade and the fan until the parade started. We wandered into his apartment, and he motioned us to a table. He served refreshments as if he were running a restaurant. The children were fascinated by his Old World hospitality. Cassetta, in turn, was impressed by their good manners.

Our unexpected arrival had interrupted Cassetta's viewing of his Italian-language TV program. With a courtesy that few native-born Americans can match, he gestured as to turn it off. I told him not to.

Emily, of course, understood some Italian and read the basic language quite fluently. Johnny, who was six, had never studied Italian, but he sometimes watched while Emily studied "Buongiorno, Italia," on PBS. And the whole family had watched a National Geographic Special about Pompeii a few weeks earlier. Johnny had also seen another PBS documentary about underwater archeology around the same time.

To Johnny's delight, the Italian-language TV show being

featured was a travelogue about the central Italian coast. His eyes lit up when he saw the familiar scenery.

"Aha! Bay of Naples, right?" he asked Cassetta, whose eyes brightened with regional pride.

"The boy speaks Italian too?"

"Not exactly," I said.

The TV screen revealed an underwater scene, showing a sunken ship, or rather, the outline of a sunken ship traced in its cargo. Johnny stared at it curiously. Few boys can resist a good shipwreck, even when it's 2,000 years old.

"Must have been a wine ship," Johnny told Cassetta.

"How you know that?" Cassetta marveled. The information had just come over the sound track in rapid-fire Italian.

"Amphorae," Johnny said, pointing to the ceramic pots sticking out of the sand. "Amphorae always means a wine ship. They're wine jars. She probably came from Greece."

"This boy is amazing," Cassetta said in Italian.

"Yeah," I said. "He watches a lot of television at home too."

Biography As History:
Role Models to Remember

Who are your child's heroes?

If a child was raised by a TV set with a little help from his or her peer group, that child probably knows that Elvis was the King and Bruce is the Boss. He or she can probably reel off the names of dozens of rock musicians, dozens of athletes, and dozens of cartoon characters.

But will that child have ever heard of Florence Nightingale or David Livingstone? For that matter, how much can that child have picked up about George Washington or Abraham Lincoln on prime-time TV or from whatever reading he or she may have been assigned in school?

Probably not very much.

Parents who nod approval while their kids make heroes and heroines out of rock stars and worship the overpaid gladiators of the spectator sports worlds as if they were pagan gods from Mount Olympus may not realize it, but they are paving the way for everything from drug abuse to premarital pregnancy to—this part should be obvious—a complete lack of interest in the academic side of school.

Rock music has a curious history. Rock was invented more or less out of whole cloth for a purely technical reason.

Once upon a time people listened to 78 rpm records that

were scratchy and broke easily. Then somebody invented 45 rpm records—the little disks with the big holes in the middle. These records had no sooner caused a retooling of phonographs and record-stamping machines than some spoilsport invented 33 rpm records that could hold ten times as much music. The new invention left people who had retooled from 78 rpm to 45 with an enormous inventory of 45 rpm equipment that nobody wanted to buy.

The people who were stuck with the 45 rpm hardware put their heads together and saved their act. They decided to create a type of music geared to short, faddish songs with primitive rhythms and melodies. To do this, they ripped off black musicians who had created a unique style of their own, retooled the same songs with white performers, and foisted the results off on teenagers through frantic advertising that relied on a kind of brutal sex appeal.

The economic avalanche this marketing touched off was bigger than anyone could have expected. The war years had discredited European classical music, and the ravenous conformity of insecure teenagers helped make rock music the only kind of music that was acceptable in high school. The kids made rock the youth anthem of the era. Classical music, once loved by educated Americans, was denigrated because so many of the composers had been German or Italian—or, in the Cold War era, Russian. You can trace the sad history of popular culture's response to classical music through Hollywood movies: before World War II, musicals frequently featured Viennese-style operetta melodies and excerpts from German or Italian composers; during the war, the German and Italian composers disappeared into an artistic limbo, and Russian composers were frantically promoted as a tribute to "our gallant Soviet allies"; when the Cold War began in 1948, Tchaikovsky and Borodin joined Wagner and Verdi in the memory hole.

Our worship of athletes as folk heroes goes back even farther, to World War I and its aftermath. Before the war, spectator sports had been a pastime for the lower classes who didn't know how to read English, and for small boys. The horrors of World War I, and the confused and chaotic peace that followed, convinced many people that politicians and politics were so corrupt and so morally depraved that sane people should give them the widest possible berth. Athletes were the heroes of the day because what they did was healthy, harmless, and anyone could keep score. They enjoyed the status that previous generations had awarded statesmen and soldiers—both now compromised because of the shambles on the Western Front.

The results of this wild upsurge in the popularity of athletes and untrained musicians had a thunderous effect on this nation's youth. "Why get an education," many young people today must ask themselves, "when people who don't have an education make a hundred times as much money playing football or the guitar as my teachers do?"

This popularity, of course, has had an effect on the athletes and entertainers as well. Many—by no means all—of the sports figures and popular musicians of earlier generations prided themselves on being good role models for kids. Today, most of them pride themselves on how much money they made last year. People who are barely literate make pronouncements on world politics, economics, and religion, and they are taken seriously by huge numbers of kids who don't know any better because they have never been told any better.

Pollsters go to the high schools. They talk to the kids. They discover that almost everybody knows which actress is living with which rock star, and that most of the boys can reel off the batting averages of dozens of baseball players. These same kids, when asked what year the Declaration of Independence was signed, don't always know the answer. Many of them place Christopher Columbus, George Washington, and Abraham Lincoln in the wrong centuries.

There have been lives in history more important than those of whoever is *hot* this month. Most kids recognize Abraham Lincoln. They've seen his picture on the five-dollar bill. But how many know anything about him as a person? My suggestion is to build a whole reading lesson around Abraham Lincoln as soon as your child is reading simple books without a great deal of struggle.

Beginning the lesson right is half the battle. A good time to start may be in early February. Ask the child to go through the newspapers, the telephone book, or maps of the area and see how many times the name *Lincoln* crops up. The child will probably come up with five or six references at the very least. Many towns have an Abraham Lincoln School. There are Lincoln Logs, and buying some might be an excellent way to mix work with play. The child can relax between reading lessons by building a log cabin of the type in which Abraham Lincoln was born.

Next, you should take not one, but several biographies of Abraham Lincoln out of the children's library. Books about Abraham Lincoln are easy to find. Typically, they will vary from super-easy readers with huge print to books from which an adult can sometimes learn. Try to pick out books that your child can read without struggle, at least for the first lesson.

Now it's time for some enrichment. A number of good movies about Abraham Lincoln are available on videotape. Two of the best are *Young Mister Lincoln* with Henry Fonda and *Abe Lincoln in Illinois* with Raymond Massey. I would show one or the other of these films *after* the child has read the easiest available book on Lincoln. Then ask the child to read another book and remember what details from the book he or she saw in the movie. This practice will train the child's critical faculty. It will also convince him or her that the text isn't an isolated collection of black words on white or yellowed paper. It's a story that relates to a real and very important life.

Now show the other movie—the one you didn't show before. Then have the child read another book. You can go on with this process until he or she becomes bored—though Lincoln will actually become a surprisingly vital and compelling figure to your child. It's worth pointing out to your children that Lincoln's formal classroom schooling lasted less than two years. He really became a lawyer and a well-read and literate man by self-imposed reading. If the child shows a strong interest, there's another vintage movie called *Abraham Lincoln* with Walter Huston. The cinematography, the sound, and some of the acting in this one are so stilted that it's almost a museum piece. But the odd thing is that the very age of the film tends to make it look almost like a documentary made during the Civil War era. I recommend it if the child shows signs of becoming a serious Lincoln enthusiast.

The key to creating a good reader is not to push the child too hard. If there's a real interest, pursue it. If the child develops a genuine fascination, let him or her continue with it. A family trip to a place associated with Lincoln's life may be an excellent investment in time and money. On the other hand, if the child is "Lincolned out" after two films and three or four books, let it slide for now.

The Fourth of July is celebrated throughout the land—and not only with fireworks and discount sales. There's no better time to begin a biographical study of George Washington or one of the other Founding Fathers. The reason I suggest beginning the biography tour with Lincoln, rather than Washington, is that there are more good films available about Lincoln. Washington, in particular, and the American Revolution, in general, haven't been hot topics with Hollywood, and several of the films that have covered the Revolutionary War have been controversial. One of the best made and least irritating films about this period of American history is *Drums Along the Mohawk,* in which Washington never appears. The picture of frontier life, the lovable characters, and the excitement make it a favorite with children, and if you can weave it into a general account of George Washington's role in history, your children will probably enjoy it and learn from it as mine did.

You can use your imagination to make this biographical tour as diverse and as graphic as possible. If you're anywhere in the original 13 colonies, a visit to a battle site or a historic home will stimulate the child to think about the way things were back then, and to do more reading about it. In any case, he or she won't just *blot out* the name or face of George Washington when he is mentioned or when his picture shows up.

Figures from history can be controversial as well as inspiring. Nobody has gone through more changes in popularity than General George Armstrong Custer. The Hollywood version has made him a hero in *They Died with Their Boots On* and *The Plainsman,* and a psychotic in *Little Big Man.* This is a good time to introduce the child to controversy and divergent opinion. You can show him or her one or more film versions about Custer, and then bring the child some books and ask the child to form his or her own opinion. (Advanced warning—some of the scenes in *Little Big Man* are gamey, and the attack on the Indian village is so gory that you may want to skip it if the child is sensitive or easily frightened.)

Another controversial figure is Napoleon Bonaparte. Napoleon is not especially well handled in American school systems. Most Americans who have heard of him remember that he was short. Such is not the case in world history, where Napoleon was a towering figure. Emily and Johnny first discovered Napoleon while we were making an off-the-air videotape of *Waterloo.* Johnny, in particular, was captivated by Rod Steiger's performance. He formed the habit of imitating Steiger imitating Napoleon—"Don't you DARE criticize me! Don't you DARE!"—during stressful moments of brother/sister relations. It was, shall we say, a way to lighten the tension.

Over a period of two or three years, Johnny read a half-dozen books about Napoleon and his era, taped several movies about Napoleon, collected Napoleonic model soldiers, and branched out from Napoleon in several directions. He also acquired a toehold on European history, a field few Americans know anything about, but one that's of great academic importance.

For Emily, a big breakthrough came with Florence Nightingale. Her first biography of Florence Nightingale led her to request more, and she branched out to learn more about the entire Victorian era. Johnny also liked reading about Florence Nightingale. In his case, reading about her heroic struggles at the hospital at Scutari fostered an interest in medicine as well as in her as a humanitarian ideal. Most people forget that Florence Nightingale, besides being a heroine to feminists and humanitarians, was a devout Christian who traced her decision to go to the Crimea to a profound religious experience. She had other religious experiences, and besides being pious and courageous, she was an excellent writer with a superb artistic sensibility.

Another eminent Victorian both children liked was David Livingstone. Our lead-in to his biography was the old feature film *Stanley and Livingstone* with Spencer Tracy and Cedric Hardwick. Livingstone's devotion to Christianity, his skills as a doctor, explorer, and scientist, and his struggle against the African slave trade made him a wonderful hero for children whose values include religious faith, racial tolerance, and courage in dealing with the strange and the unexpected. Another familiar figure in the children's biographical studies was General Charles Gordon, whose struggle against the slave trade was also motivated by a deep if unconventional Christian faith. Good books about Gordon aren't easy to find, but there are three excellent movies that cover his life: *Khartoum* with Charlton Heston and Laurence Olivier, *The Four Feathers* with John Clements and Ralph Richardson, and *Young Winston* with Simon Ward, Robert Shaw, and Anne Bancroft. Bracketed together, these movies not only introduce children to another world figure—Winston Churchill—but display the panoply of the British Empire and the British society they will encounter later in literature and history classes in high school and college.

Using biography to teach history, and using both biography and history to encourage recreational reading and critical thinking, can break the habit of worshiping commercially concocted heroes and blaming all of one's troubles on concocted villains forever. The possibilities for *quality time* between parent and child are also important. I have to say, frankly, that I really don't care anything about New Kids on the Block. And my interest in the over-publicized screen antics of Batman, Dick Tracy, and the Teenage Mutant Ninja Turtles wore out very, very quickly. I further suspect that none of those worthies will ever turn up on an SAT test or as a college essay assignment.

On the other hand, I will never forget how excited Johnny was when the Metropolitan Museum of Art featured costumes from the age of Napoleon. Emily was bedazzled by the elegant empire gowns and the jewelry, but that didn't surprise me. At 12, she was a long-established member of the culturati. I thrilled to watch Johnny tearing around the exhibits, so fast, in many cases, he barely had a chance to study anything in detail.

"Look at this! His tent! His own bed! This is unbelievable! Look at these uniforms! Who says all Frenchmen are short! This grenadier must have been at least six feet!"

The same kid who had to be pried out of the Napoleon exhibit with a crow bar pronounced that his social studies course in school was his least favorite subject.

"Social studies," he mused glumly. "I guess that means history with all the people taken out of it. That must be why it's so boring."

Reading Foreign Languages for Fun

As you near the third-year mark in your child's home school-ing, you've probably discovered that you're running out of things to do in your foreign-language program. Your child, if he or she has gone over the lessons in *See It and Say It* and the Lee Cooper *Fun with...* books probably knows just about every word by heart. If your child is a quick learner, he or she may even have read all the easy picture books in the French, German, or Spanish section of the children's room at the library.

Boredom does not make learning easier. If it did, the public schools would not be in such trouble. Children learn best when they're excited, challenged—even amused, if the amusement doesn't break down into time-wasting and disrup-tive noise.

There are some ways to keep your foreign-language stu-dent interested and not bored. All it takes is a little bit of energy, a little bit of time, and maybe—but not invariably—a little bit of money.

Here are some ideas to keep your supplemental foreign language program a fiesta, instead of a siesta.

Go on a foreign-language scavenger hunt!
Your own public library, unless it's a big one, probably

doesn't have more than a half-dozen foreign-language children's books in any given language. Pack the kids into the car or bus and try some other libraries. You will find that children's libraries don't always have the same five books. The kids and I located a whole collection of Walt Disney easy-readers in French at a library a few miles from our home. At another, we found a Spanish-language biography, with color illustrations, of the Argentine liberator Jose San Martin, several French children's books on Joan of Arc, a French children's book of etiquette with delightfully funny illustrations from the 1920s, and French biographies of Napoleon and Cardinal Richelieu, as well as books about animals. Also on hand were the classic French children's stories by Alphonse Daudet and Victor Hugo, and a historically fascinating propaganda piece by Hansi, a French Alsatian. Hansi describes blond Alsatian children journeying to the beautiful lands of central France. They're promptly set upon by a wicked knight with a red brush-cut and turned-up moustache, and a black eagle stamped on his chest. Guess which country he represents? Hansi points up the motto as two handsome French knights drive the villain away:

"Never forget, little Alsatians, if you speak the language of the *Boche,* he'll think you're his serfs. Be sure to speak French!"

You never know what you're going to find when you go to a new library. By exploring, the child will pick up the habit of going to a library, and he or she may encounter all the other worthwhile things that go on at libraries—concerts, lectures, art exhibits, and displays of keepsakes and memorabilia. It's a habit that should last a lifetime.

If your library has an interloan system, you can take some of the books out on an interlibrary card. If not, you can read them on the spot. Remember that the variety of new places, provided they aren't threatening or seriously disappointing, will always stimulate the child to extra effort. And while your own library may not have more than 5 or 6 books in any given language, you can probably have access to 50 to 100 different children's books if you have an intercounty card.

Build a model with foreign instructions!

Most men have fond memories of building model airplanes, ships, or racing cars when they were boys. Some men retain the habit through life. It's a therapeutic hobby that father and son can enjoy together—and some girls enjoy building and painting models too.

If you explore hobby shops or the larger toy stores, you will notice that some of the models have foreign flags printed on the color illustrations on the boxes. These flags mean that the assembly instructions are included in foreign languages.

You can have a lot of fun—and maybe a bit of a challenge— if you buy one of these models and try to put it together using the instructions in the language you've studied. This effort may be more fun than you suspect. Don't expect the model to come out picture-perfect. Your problems, however, may be small ones since whatever text you have to puzzle out will be fully illustrated. This activity will be especially valuable if it enables parents and children to share some quality time together while sharing a learning experience. Plastic models are also useful because they're a visual aid in teaching principles of engineering, as well as recent history. Building plastic models should not become a substitute for reading, but it's a welcome substitute for too much TV viewing.

See what kinds of literature are available in foreign languages!

You would probably be surprised to discover how many products come with dual-language instructions, either English/French or English/Spanish, or sometimes even with four-language instructions in English, French, German, and Spanish. This is a made-to-order situation for some impromptu translating. I've found bilingual and trilingual instructions on everything from my (American-made) automobile to posters in the post office. Showing these instructions to your son or daughter will help point up the fact that it's not an entirely English-speaking world. The child will also have some fun figuring out which words match in the translations even if the student can't provide a letter-perfect translation.

Another good place to look for bilingual or trilingual texts is on food labels, especially of imported or gourmet food items. How much gourmet or imported food you buy depends on your tastes and your budget. But if you buy any at all, you're wasting an opportunity if you don't allow the child to try to translate the foreign texts on the labels even if they only include a few words.

Which brings us to another subject . . . Have dinner at a foreign restaurant!

Are there any restaurants in your region that have menus in foreign languages—without translations? You can have a lot of fun, and validate your emphasis on learning a foreign language if you find a restaurant that offers menus in the language your child has studied. If he or she can explain the menu to the rest of the family, exchange salutations with the waiter or waitress, and enjoy the food and ambience of a restaurant with the help of a knowledge of French, Spanish, Italian, or German, the child may be *hooked* on the language for life. This experience will have a wonderful influence not only on his or her academic progress, but on that priceless quality—self-confidence.

Look for foreign-language pen pals!

Many children, especially girls but boys too, enjoy having pen pals in other countries. You can write to the consulates or embassies of foreign countries or to various international pen-pal groups to find pen pals for your child, or to create a pen-pal relationship with a family in another country. Some churches also maintain active contacts with churches in other countries. Many people around the world—contrary to what you may have heard—actually like Americans and are fascinated by the American way of life. My daughter, simply through networking, has acquired pen pals in Canada, Germany, Japan, South Africa, Czechoslovakia, the Soviet Union, and the Falkland Islands, as well as in Michigan, Missouri, and California.

The advantages in later life that can be acquired through the habit of letter-writing can range from simple secretarial work to journalism or legal correspondence. This practice has already appeared in Emily's ability to express herself in written school assignments, at which she excels. Most of the children who write to the United States from overseas want to practice their English; and many of them, who don't speak English at home, started studying in school when they were in the early years of grade school, which is the key to their success in learning English. But there's no reason why the flow of knowledge should always be out of the country: Emily and her pen pal in Germany always split the letters, writing half of each letter in English and half in German.

Reread classic children's stories in the original languages!

There's a real advantage to having a child read the classic children's stories by Jacob and Wilhelm Grimm or by Charles Perrault. Once they know the stories in English, they may want to enjoy them in the language in which they were written.

Perrault's writings have an immense charm in the pure French of the 1600s—"The Great Century," as the French call it. While the spellings have been harmonized to modern usage in any version that's commercially available in the United States, there's very little change from the way Charles Perrault actually set these stories down when he was writing them for Louis XIV's court. If your child has been reading simple French for two or three years, if he or she already knows the stories in plot and outline, and if he or she knows how to use a dictionary, you will be surprised, I think, at how well your child will take to them.

The same is true of the Grimm stories in German, which are even simpler in style and extremely vital. There's one caution: make sure that the version of the Brothers Grimm that you give your home schooler to read is in High German. Most children's editions will be, but the original edition of *Kinder und Hausmärchen* is a museum of German dialects, and the child who picks up this copy will have trouble spotting words, let alone making out the stories. Remember that Jacob and Wilhelm Grimm were collecting these stories to preserve the dialects as well as the tales themselves. A professional philologist or a native-born German with a good imagination may be able to read all the stories in the Grimms' original version with understanding. Your child won't. Get a version that's in modern German.

Bring the Bible into your foreign language course!

John Quincy Adams, one of the brightest men ever to occupy the White House, had a hobby that was characteristically and uniquely his own: he used to read the Bible to himself in different foreign languages before going to sleep. Adams was a wonderful linguist. His translations of the Roman poet Horace are an absolute romp, and he enjoyed doing them so much that they often contain twice as many stanzas as the original. But he hit on a very practical idea. He knew the Bible quite well, of course, but by exploring a familiar story in a foreign language, he learned seven or eight languages much more pleasantly than he would have by plowing through endless grammars and overly simple stories for beginners.

You can use this idea in your own home schooling. Once your child has learned the rudiments of the Bible, and has read the Gospels at least once in English, you can bring the Bible into your foreign-language program as a text, which combines solid spiritual values with stories that never grow old and wear out.

The child who forms the habit of reading ten or twelve verses of the Bible daily in a language they have been learning for two years or more, and then moves up to an entire chapter a day by the third year, will combine daily Bible reading with a skill that's mind-expanding even as it's soul-strengthening. You can order a Bible in any major language from any good Christian bookstore. No other book contains so many stories that will appeal to both children and adults on every level.

Most parents of public-school children would be delighted

to be able to introduce Bible lessons and messages into the curriculum. Many would also love to introduce a foreign language at an age when children can still absorb one effectively. Your supplemental program, done in less than a half hour a day, can combine both Bible and foreign language in a way that will build a lifelong literacy in French or German with a familiarity with the most important book of all time.

ELEVEN

The Humanities Program from a Christian Perspective

Cultural illiteracy has become a "hot" issue in many upscale school districts around the country as parents and teachers discover that even upper-middle-class kids don't know anything about world history, art, or culture. Adults who attended school in the 1940s or 1950s gag at the mention of high school graduates and college freshmen who can't place George Washington, Abraham Lincoln, or Christopher Columbus in their proper centuries. Dates beyond the Declaration of Independence are a murky mystery to many college applicants. The solution, of course, is not to mandate a wider knowledge by the students—it's to water down the entry standards so youngsters can keep attending colleges and to protect the job security of the professors and administrators.

Everyone has his own favorite horror stories. Mine include the Harvard graduate in Soviet studies who couldn't understand the simplest phrases in Russian, the Princeton American history major who had never been told that Congress had to ratify Indian treaties, and the Harvard history major who didn't know that Germany had been a unified country in the Middle Ages and had been, in fact, the single most powerful country in Europe for about 600 years prior to the Reformation. This worthy graduate of what purports to be the most

117

prestigious university in the United States, needless to say, couldn't speak a word of German, which is a critical skill in his major. And his attempts to pronounce German words from academic conversationalese were a source of scandalized amusement to those who had received an education, as opposed to a diploma. Lest we forget the other leg of the Ivy League tripod, I remember the Yale man who edited the word *spleen* into *spine* in one of my stories. He didn't realize that there was a human organ called a spleen and assumed that I didn't know how to spell *spine*. This same editor, a fine arts major, didn't know a single word of Italian. It was as if the Renaissance had never happened! I wonder if he actually knew what he was looking at, anatomically or culturally, during all those years of staring at paintings.

There's a way to nip cultural illiteracy in the bud. It doesn't involve sending the student, now in his twenties, for yet another college diploma—in Europe—so he or she can learn about American history.

The solution is to take home schooling "to the movies." Television is a major cause of cultural illiteracy because it takes up most of the time that children (and adults) of previous generations used to spend reading. Yet it can cure, as well as cause, cultural illiteracy. Television has one great strength: Because it's so intensely visual, it can reach children vividly. The problem you will face as a teacher is to reach them with the information you want them to have.

Your campaign against cultural illiteracy consists of three steps: Find the right movie to interest the child in a subject; find the right books to offer further information; and then have the child compare and contrast the movie and the book. The compare-and-contrast session will be verbal if the child is young. When you are home supplementing an older child, or most especially if you've bitten the bullet and are home schooling full time, you will find this program is a great way to inspire writing exercises that provide a chance to teach the student spelling, punctuation, and organization. Most important of all, it keeps the child in the habit of reading to confirm and expand information from a visual source.

How do you know which books and movies to match? I'll share with you how I did it, leaving out a few of my mistakes and mentioning only those films and movies that worked together well for me. In my case, since I was home schooling, I broke the film-book interaction up into chronological order, showing the films and assigning the books as they happened in the course of history. If you're supplement-teaching, you can do this activity by showing one film per weekend on Friday night, with reading assigned Saturday and Sunday to avoid clashing with school homework.

The first film in my series was *The Ten Commandments* with Charlton Heston and Yul Brynner. I know this film has been criticized as an overdone spectacle, but I'm considering each film as a supplemental teaching aid, not a deathless work of cinematic art. Most of the films I recommend can be criticized on some basis or other, but they have two advantages: they're widely available in video shops, and they introduce students to an important era of history.

Once the student has seen *The Ten Commandments,* you're ready to introduce "the print version." I suggest two Bible story books both my children enjoyed, *Bible Stories For Children,* retold by Geoffrey Horn and Arthur Cavanaugh, and *Egermeier's Bible Story Book* by Elsie Egermeier, with revisions by Arlene S. Hall. The Egermeier book may be out of print, but it's available in both church and public libraries, and the Horn-Cavanaugh book is widely available at libraries and bookstores.

While using the books, you should discuss Israel's presence in Egypt. This study includes the Bible stories of Joseph and his brothers through the story of Moses and the Exodus. The best way to handle this activity is to show the film on the first day of your seminar and to have your student read the stories at a comfortable pace over the next few days. Obviously, you can't start this course before your student is reading fluently. I started Emily at the age of six, and Johnny at the age of seven, commencing the course at the beginning of the school year in September.

If the child seems interested in Egypt or the ancient Egyptians, you may want to expand this part of the course. The nicest thing about home education, and the reason it works so much better than mass classroom instruction, is that you can change your schedule to pursue the child's personal preferences in anything that's wholesome or important. The only thing to remember is never to lose sight of the basics—but by now you've covered them already and have plenty of time for enrichment. A number of books about Egypt are available at most children's libraries. There are also two other feature films, *Land of the Pharaohs* and *The Egyptian*, which are sometimes available in video rental. Both were thought somewhat "steamy" in the era when they were made, but by modern standards they're actually quite tame in terms of both sex and violence. If you can use them to promote a wider interest in Egyptian history, art, and culture, I don't think they will corrupt the child.

The next stop is ancient Greece, which was the starting point of all European civilization as we understand it. The Greeks appear regularly in high school and, especially, in college and university courses.

The first film I would recommend is *Clash of the Titans*. Some aspects of this film may seem downright silly to adults, and Laurence Olivier took his critical lumps for appearing in it as a very tired-looking Zeus, but kids find the movie gripping. (I know because once when I was out of the house and their mother was gardening, they put the tape on by themselves—after they had just seen it!) The special effects— winged horses that fly, giant monsters, three-headed dogs, women with snakes in their hair—are straight out of Greek mythology.

The believability of Greek stories is an important issue to raise with children: the Greek myths, unlike the Bible, are not *history*, but *mythology*. The stories of mythological monsters that couldn't possibly have existed are very different from Bible stories about real men and women whose lives were touched by God. The giants in the Bible were very large men, not monsters taller than a 10-story building. Children need to be told early the difference between Greek and Roman mythology and biblical history so they aren't taken in by modern "myth-makers" who try to promote the lie that the Bible is only a collection of fairy tales. For your own information on this subject, you may want to consult *The Bible As History* by Werner Keller. The author shows how an improved knowledge of world history through archeology and the translation of ancient languages fits history's version given in the Bible so precisely that attempts to portray the Bible as a *myth* quickly become ridiculous. *The Bible As History* is probably too difficult for everyone except the brightest children of pre-high school years. No Christian home teaching parent, however, should overlook this book for his or her own information or the child's.

Clash of the Titans, whatever its lack of artistic merits, points up the huge contrast between the God of the Bible and the gods of ancient Greece. The Greek gods are too human— sometimes silly. They're the best that humanity could come up with purely through imagination. The concept of a just and righteous God, embodied in the Bible, was absolutely necessary before Western civilization could develop in the way that it has. Children should understand this fact as early as possible. It's the core of a Christian approach to the humanities.

After you have introduced the Greek gods and heroes with *Clash of the Titans,* it's time for the reading. The two best books for children I found readily available are *D'Aulaire's Book of Greek Myths,* by Ingri and Edgar Parin D'Aulaire, and *The MacMillan Book of Greek Gods and Heroes,* by Alice Low, illustrated by Arvis Stewart. Any children's library will almost certainly have copies of both, and they are both still in print. Children love both these books. I know because after Johnny had looked through the copy I bought for Emily, he bought one for himself—with his own pocket money. That was a strong endorsement.

Clash of the Titans is based on myth. The story of Odysseus, however, is a mixture of myth and legend. We don't believe in Zeus any more, but archeologists now know that Troy was a real place and not a fairy-tale kingdom, and that an ancient Greek army actually looted and burned it. The film about this subject you're most likely to be able to find is *Ulysses (Odysseus)* with Kirk Douglas. The action in this one is nonstop, and the art director actually did his homework: The costumes, sets, and props are a fusion of Greek archaic and classical styles that fit the mood perfectly. Even roughneck boys who don't care too much for art will find the scenes with the Cyclops irresistible. For months after we saw this film together, Johnny would do Cyclops imitations. We watched *Ulysses* about the time that his front baby teeth came out, and Johnny, already sensitive enough to know that he looked a bit like a monster without front teeth, soothed himself by talking like the Cyclops. When he showed his gapped gums, he would suck in his breath and gasp out, "What do you find so amusing?" in a deep, rasping voice, bending his head forward in a baleful glowering expression. It *was* genuinely amusing, and if the Cyclops ever turns up on a school test, Johnny will be the first to remember who (or what) he (or it) was.

Odysseus' story may be found, in brief, in the later sections of both the D'Aulaire and MacMillan books. You can also locate a number of books about Odysseus and the Trojan War at most children's libraries. I would recommend you let children read about this subject until they're "read out." Make sure the books you pick out for them, or with them, aren't so far beyond their reading level that they come to dislike the story in particular or reading in general. The guideline here is the same as it was for stimulating early reading. If the child stumbles over more than five or six words on any given page, the book is too difficult for him or her right now. Six months or a year in the future, it may be perfect. Let it wait until then.

The main point to make comparing *Ulysses* to *Clash of the Titans* is the difference between *myth* and *legend*. A *myth* is a purely fictional story, often made up to explain some natural event. A *legend* is a story that might once have been true, made bigger than life in the retelling. *Clash of the Titans* is a myth. Children can clearly perceive this because of the unreal monsters and because pagan gods are central to the story. *Ulysses* is a legend. There was a real city of Troy. There may have been a real man like Ulysses (Odysseus). Some of the details that involve magic or monsters were later made up. The difference between myth and legend is usually covered in senior high school or college, but there's no reason why a student can't start to understand the difference when he or she is still a child.

Most children enjoy Greek myths and legends. If you want to expand beyond the basics, you might do something really daring and show the children some of the old Steve Reeves "Hercules" movies. I know to some purists these films represent the ultimate corruption of classical mythology into sort of "muscle-beach movies with monsters." But we're not dealing with art critics. And if you think the Hercules movies are bad, consider the kind of junk that teenagers watch almost compulsively to see who can take the most gore and gristle without running out of the theatre or away from the TV set. Stories about Hercules are in both the D'Aulaire and the MacMillan book, and separate books are available at children's libraries. Your child will probably read them without objecting. Johnny loved reading about Hercules, and even Emily found the stories enjoyable, especially the ones that involved a certain amount of humor.

After the children have read about Hercules, check out a video, if you can find one, of *Samson and Delilah* with Victor Mature and Hedy Lamarr. The children will enjoy this film even if adults find some of it a bit grandiose. You should then have the children read about Samson in the Bible story books.

An important compare-and-contrast possibility is here between Hercules and Samson. Hercules, a figure of myth, fought against all sorts of monsters. Samson, a man of history, fought against evil or misguided human beings. Children need to understand that while Hercules is a wonderful character of fiction, he never really lived. They should also understand that Hercules and Samson were both undone by the misuse of their own muscles. The husky boy who is tempted to shirk his studies in favor of an obsession with sports—or worse yet, with bullying other children—should remember that neither the mythical Hercules nor the biblical Samson ever found happiness through the abuse of brute strength.

From Greek myths and legends, move on to Greek history. There's a film that can introduce this topic: *The 300 Spartans* with Richard Egan and Ralph Richardson. This movie is about 300 Spartan warriors who were killed to the last man defending the pass at Thermopylae from a Persian invasion. The story is a legend central to European (or Western) history, but there's no doubt at all that it actually happened. The film tends to glorify the Spartans a little too much; they were heroic, as the film shows, but they were also fascists. But it's a vital part of every child's cultural education to know what words like *Spartan* and *democracy* mean, to see Greek democracy in debate, and to understand that not every hero comes back alive.

The book that augments this film perfectly is *Lion in the Gateway,* by Mary Renault. The reading level may be a bit demanding, but it *is* a book for young people, and the subject is worth the effort. The book, in fact, is required reading because the film ends with the defeat of the Spartans by the Persians, and the child has to remember that they weren't just a bunch of good soldiers who were killed, but the heroes who saved Western democracy. The book goes on to describe the Greek victories over the Persians that drove them back into Asia and saved Europe. If the child sees the movie, he or she will probably read *The Lion in the Gateway* voluntarily. If there's a real interest, and if the child's reading level is good, an excellent supplement is *Tales from Herodotus,* by Fairfax Downey. Herodotus, as everybody used to know a hundred years ago, was the Father of History. His book, *The Persian*

Wars, is not just an account of the battles between Greece and Persia, but a description of the known world. Fairfax Downey's fine collection of stories encapsules the same stories Mary Renault tells in *Lion in the Gateway,* but offers them in a simplified straight translation of Herodotus. It's a wonderful introduction to classical history for the child with a solid reading ability and just a little patience.

The next film brings Greek history to a climax. It's *Alexander the Great* with Richard Burton and Fredric March. The film contains enough fighting to keep even a roughhouse specialist on the edge of his chair, and the plot, despite the "sword-and-sandal" costumes, is sophisticated enough to hold an adult's interest. The costumes, in fact, led many critics to undervalue the serious worth of this movie when it was released. (The undertones of adultery, latent incest, and bisexuality in the rather sophisticated screenplay will go right over the heads of pre-high schoolers.)

The companion volume to this movie is *Alexander the Great,* by John Gunther. This book will introduce your home schooler to the world of Landmark Books. The Landmark series, now out of print, are large-print, high-interest biographies of important men and women from world history or American history. These, and the similar but slightly easier Signature books, were victims of the public school's pronounced failure to teach students to read early enough to keep books like these viable. When they were written, they were intended for preadolescents, children 8 to 12 years old. Most children in that age-range today don't read well enough to understand Landmark and Signature Books. By the time they *do* read well enough, they want books that are "spicy" — and the Landmark and Signature series, like the similar Credo series published under the auspices of the Catholic Church, are morally sound and scrupulously free of sexual enticement. They're also historically accurate. The books are preserved, I suspect, by children's librarians who learned to love them as children in the 1950s and can't bear to see them destroyed.

Once you have your home schooler involved with Landmark and Signature books, you're on solid ground. Gunther's
Alexander the Great is a good book to start with. Johnny, at
the point we reached it, was not a voracious reader, but he
absorbed a lot from it. I also gave him another Landmark
book, this one without a film tie-in, from roughly the same
era: *The Exploits of Xenophon,* retold by Geoffrey Household.
This book is a shortened English translation of *The Anabasis,*
one of the books once familiar to every student of classical
Greek. I wasn't sure how much of it Johnny actually remembered. But six months later, he saw an Indian at a powwow
brace his foot against a bow-stave to string a bow, and he
started to talk about how the Kurds, fighting against the
Greeks and Persians, would brace one foot against their bow-
staves when shooting arrows that would pierce armor. Nobody who heard this account at the powwow had the slightest
idea of what Johnny was talking about, but I knew that he had
absorbed more from Xenophon than I had thought.

The world of the Greeks and the world of the Bible are the
two foundations of an understanding of the humanities. No
one who has started to explore them as a child stands in
much danger of becoming a cultural illiterate. But it was
during the Roman period that these two streams merged to
create the distinctive culture of Western Europe. That's the
next goal of our excursion.

There's a point to be made in teaching children about the
Roman world that's especially important to Christian boys
and girls. A knowledge of Roman history allows the Christian
child to understand the importance of Jesus in His historical
as well as spiritual context.

The world in which Jesus was born was the early Roman
Empire. But before there was a Roman Empire, there was a
Roman Republic, which played a major role in the thinking of
the Founding Fathers of the United States.

The best film introduction to the Roman Republic shows
the republic already crumbling: The film is *Spartacus* with
Kirk Douglas. Rightly hailed as the thinking man's epic, the

movie depicts the revolt of gladiators and slaves against their Roman masters. It is not, in fact, a Christian film, since it takes place a hundred years before the Resurrection. But *Spartacus* offers a vivid picture of human values in the century before Jesus, besides describing an actual historic event. A little knowledge of the Roman world is indeed a dangerous thing to the antireligious community. I once listened to an atheist launch into an attack on Christianity by attempting to tell his audience that the Romans never really crucified people. The climax of *Spartacus*, based on information from pre-Christian Roman historians, refutes this attack with horrific force. So too do the writings of Cicero, among other Roman writers, but that's beyond the purview of basic home schooling.

Once *Spartacus* has dramatically introduced the Romans, it's time to start the reading. One good general introduction is *The Romans*, by Alfred Duggan. Many illustrated books about Roman life and culture are also available at children's libraries.

The period just before the Christian era was the age of Julius Caesar, born in 100 B.C. and assassinated in 44 B.C. on the Ides of March, as every reader of Shakespeare must remember. This, by the way, is a good time to introduce Shakespeare with the superb black-and-white film version of Shakespeare's *Julius Caesar*, starring James Mason as Brutus and Marlon Brando as Mark Anthony. You may not believe it, but my kids actually sat through this film, and claimed to have enjoyed it — at least to the extent that they were glued to the screen.

"When are they going to kill him?" Johnny kept asking. (He'd already read one account of Caesar's assassination in another book.)

The book to follow this film is another Landmark book, *Julius Caesar*, by John Gunther. Even an adult can learn a great deal from reading this book, which is true of Landmark books in general. I confess I filled in some of the potholes in my own education, or at least refreshed my memory by reading along with the children to make sure they were really doing their work.

So far there haven't been many books geared especially to girls on our program, and the Landmark book on *Cleopatra,* by Elizabeth Hornblow, is reading for both boys and girls. They will all like it. Emily, in fact, loved it and reread it voluntarily a few months after her first reading. I suspect she had absorbed enough Christianity not to take on Cleopatra as a role model.

One companion film to this reading was *Cleopatra* — not the splashy and scandal-ridden version with Elizabeth Taylor and Richard Burton, but the older black-and-white film with Claudette Colbert, which is a little hokey but a whole lot of fun. For good measure, if you can find it, there's a color version of George Bernard Shaw's *Caesar and Cleopatra* with Claude Rains and Vivian Leigh, a witty costume epic well worth seeing for the crackling dialogue, even though neither Caesar nor Cleopatra is depicted with total accuracy. The film approach, coupled with the reading, worked particularly well in this case. When the Brooklyn Museum held an exhibit on Anthony and Cleopatra, Emily, now back in school, asked her teacher for permission to skip a day so we could all go see it. The teacher asked me about this request and mentioned how surprised she was that anybody Emily's age even knew who Cleopatra was.

"Her brother put her up to it," I said. "He wanted to see it too."

"Oh," the teacher said. "Her older brother. I didn't think a sixth-grader would have been interested in Cleopatra by herself."

"Her brother's just turned eight," I said quietly. Conversation sort of flagged after that.

A study of the Nativity should follow shortly after the demise of Anthony and Cleopatra. There are, of course, any number of movies about the life of Jesus. My own personal favorite is Franco Zeffirelli's *Jesus of Nazareth* with Robert Powell. No film is immune to criticism, and I can spot several mistakes in this one if I'm pressed to it. But the sincerity of the performances, and the near-miraculous achievement of making a film that's powerfully Christian and pro-Jewish at the same time, with even a few touches of humanity in individual Romans, makes *Jesus of Nazareth* a masterpiece. The clear message is that Jesus was not crucified by "the Jews" or "the Romans" but by a small power-ridden clique drawn from both groups is a strong recommendation. I also liked the fact that the Resurrection is depicted as taking place in time and space, and not just "in the hearts of His friends." Aside from any question of faith, I personally believe that only a genuine Resurrection could explain where a group of very ordinary fishermen and peasants found the courage to challenge first the Jewish establishment, and then the Roman Empire—and eventually, to win.

The struggle between the Romans and the Christians is depicted in several spectacular movies that were sometimes disparaged by critics, but have won a warm spot in my heart as a home schooling parent. I recommend both *The Robe* and its sequel, *Demetrius and the Gladiators,* as a sort of cultural entertainment event. People who enjoy irony say *The Robe* is worth watching simply to see Victor Mature, supposedly a muscleman, outact Richard Burton, who had Shakespearean experience before he descended on Hollywood. Both films may be a little pious for modern tastes, but children love them. Names like *Caligula, Claudius,* and *Messalina,* once part of every cultured person's vocabulary, still a staple of tests on advanced European history, can be introduced vividly. And is there any better way to introduce a child to Nero— at a safe distance—than with *Quo Vadis?* This movie too has risen in critics' esteem. No student of either the early church or the Roman Empire should miss it. Children should be shown one of the key points: Petronius and his friends, the last bearers of the old Roman culture, are unable to stand up to Nero's evil insanity. But the Christians, despite terrible persecution, *do* prevail in the end. The spectacle and the decor of the film speak for themselves.

The viewing of these films should be accompained by New Testament stories direct from the Bible. I would suggest by this time that the child read the Gospels and the Acts of the Apostles in a good large-print modern edition. Two fine Landmark books are also on the New Testament, *Jesus of Nazareth* and *The Life of Paul,* both by Harry Emerson Fosdick. It's vital for children to understand the historicity of Jesus and Paul to insulate them against the secular-humanist lie that Jesus was a mythical figure and that Paul "invented" Him. (I know it sounds absurd to any believing Christian, but your child will encounter this sort of propaganda when he becomes a teenager or college student.)

The Fall of the Roman Empire is an appropriate conclusion to ancient history. One of the last big-screen epics, this film focuses on the shift of power from the stoic Roman Emperor Marcus Aurelius (Alex Guinness) to his mad son Commodus (Christopher Plummer). Real and fictional characters are intertwined in an account of why Rome fell that is condensed and simplistic, but extremely provocative. The sets and costumes are a marvel. The film also offers a look at the Germanic barbarians, which is not completely negative or hostile. Perhaps the most lovable character in the entire movie is the Greek freedman played by James Mason, who turns out to be a secret Christian and who sacrifices his life for his beliefs. (You can see the Chi-Rho symbol of the early Christian church when Stephen Boyd turns Mason over after he has been killed.)

The book to read in concert with *The Fall of the Roman Empire* is *The First Book of the Barbarian Invaders,* by Donald Sobol. It's important to remind children that the Germanic barbarians were the ancestors not only of the modern Germans, Austrians, and Swiss, but of the English, the Lowland Scots, the Dutch, and the northern French, and that they played an ancestral role in northern Italy and northern Spain as well. Most Americans who trace their ancestry to Northern or Central Europe are their direct descendants. These people were farmers and herdspeople rather than city builders and scholars when the Romans encountered them, but they certainly weren't cavepeople or ape-like primitives. Their language can easily be recognized as the ancestor of modern German—and, combined with the Latin of the Romans, as the ancestor of modern English.

You should also point out that missionaries had already Christianized most of them when they settled down in Roman territories, and that they tended to intermarry with the Romans and Celts who had already lived there instead of killing them, as many past historians once believed. All Western culture is a fusion of these three elements: Greek and Roman, Celtic and Germanic, and Christian. And Christianity made the fusion possible. Another fine Landmark book about this era is *The Life of Saint Patrick,* by Quentin Reynolds. The better readers should also check out *Charlemagne* by Manuel Komroff. Unfortunately, I don't know of any film tie-ins for either of these important books.

Few children can resist the Middle Ages, once they learn about the days of knights and fair ladies, kings and queens, and castles dotting the landscape. The era is recalled in many fairy tales, but it had a historical reality that also needs to be recognized.

The first film-book combination I would recommend is the film *Knights of the Round Table* with Robert Taylor and the Landmark book *King Arthur and His Knights,* by Mabel L. Robinson. I'll never forget the expression on Emily's face when she looked up from the book and said: "Hey! I actually *like* these stories."

The next pairing is the movie *The Vikings* with Kirk Douglas and Tony Curtis and *The Vikings,* by Elizabeth Janeway. The movie, described in *TV Guide* as "incredible Norse mayhem," won't have any trouble capturing even a rambunctious boy's attention. Johnny was frozen to the screen when we watched it.

"Are there still Vikings?" he asked leerily.

"No," I said.

He shuddered with relief. Then he got curious.

"What happened to them?" he asked.

"They gave up on that sort of thing when they became Christians," I said.

"Boy!" Johnny said, still staring at the screen. "I guess they had to."

The Janeway book, as a sequel to the movie, will show how Christianity replaced the old Norse religion and converted the bloodthirsty sea raiders into settlers and explorers. The book's main topic is the Viking voyages to North America. The child who shows a serious interest in Viking culture may also want to read the D'Aulaire book on Norse myths, or one of the many illustrated books about Vikings in children's libraries.

The Normans, as their name would suggest, were direct descendants of the Norsemen, and their story appears in *William the Conqueror*, a Landmark book by Thomas B. Costain. I don't know of any widely available film about the Norman conquest of England in 1066. But two films, both classics, cover the aftermath: *The Adventures of Robin Hood* with Errol Flynn, and *Ivanhoe* with Robert Taylor. The spinoffs I would suggest from these two rousing movies are *The Crusades* by Anthony West, and *The Magna Carta*, by James Daugherty, both in the Landmark series.

No look at the Middle Ages is complete without the stories of *Joan of Arc*, a Landmark book by Nancy Wilson Ross, and *The Adventures and Discoveries of Marco Polo*, by Richard J. Walsh. For good—or bad—measure, you may want to add *Genghis Khan*, by Harold Lamb. There's nothing wrong with the way the book is written, but hero worship of conquering rulers is a tendency in most small boys. You will probably want to explain that slaughtering large numbers of defenseless people has never made anyone a truly great person.

The end of the Middle Ages came with Constantinople's fall, as described in *The Fall of Constantinople*, a Landmark book by Bernardine Kielty. I know of no film account of this crucial event, but the book is worth reading on its own. I have fond memories of my freshman year in an honors English class, taught by a Rhodes Scholar who could read Anglo-Saxon: He asked the class of 30, who were the brightest students on the campus, to tell him in what year Constantinople had fallen to the Turks. I was the only one who even knew in what century we were dealing. I learned about it from Kielty's elegaic and striking book.

By now we are back on familiar terrain—the ground we covered in teaching children to love reading through biographies of famous men and women. A quick look at an encyclopedia, or the biography itself, will show in what era the biography is set. You may want to continue in historical sequence, or concentrate on specific times or people. But you've turned a major corner in fighting cultural illiteracy and fostering a lifetime of good reading if you've convinced the child that reading history and historical biography is a better way to spend time than paging through cheap fiction and gossipy books about movie stars and rock singers.

And you've probably had a good time doing it.

TWELVE

Learning That Never Ends

By the time you've completed the humanities program, your child will probably be about 10 years old. At this point, if the child has kept up with the lesson plan in this book, he or she is probably just about failure-proofed. The various tests the public schools dole out in such full measure will also probably tell you—if you've used the methods in the book to establish early an avid reading and a solid base in math—that the child is well ahead of most of his or her peers.

By the time the child is 9 or 10, whether in or out of school, he or she should be branching out in math to do long division, detailed fractions with the lowest common denominator, decimals, and the calculating of the areas and volumes of regular shapes. If you don't remember how to do these things yourself, ask a professional teacher or somebody you know who's good in math, or look up the Golden *Step Ahead* books available in most stationery stores.

You can also get some help from a Little Professor. This educational toy really educates. It's a very simple portable computer, about the size of a small book, that asks the child to solve math problems by pushing keys, and tells the child when he or she is right or wrong.

"I loved this thing the first time I saw it," Johnny said of his Little Professor. "It was like having my own robot."

Much as he might groan when told to answer two or three pages of math lessons, he almost never complained when told to bang out a few "10s" (perfect scores) on his Little Professor. He became so good at it that anything less than a "10" became something of a disgrace—and something of a rarity.

The third- and fourth-grade years are also the time to move into penmanship and the study of formal grammar. Again, if you don't remember grammar from your own schooling, you can find books and booklets that will help you teach the child the parts of speech and sentence diagramming. I don't suggest tackling this level before the child is 9 or 10 and a fluent reader because too much emphasis on English formalities may make the child dislike reading. It's like learning to eat. You don't sit the child down at a dinner table with fancy linen and porcelain and three kinds of forks and spoons while they're still learning to chew solid food and drink out of a cup instead of a nipple. On the other hand, you don't want to delay penmanship and grammar beyond the age of 10 because the child retains things better when they're learned early.

One of the best ways to introduce formal grammar and the parts of speech is by diagramming. Some teachers stressed, or even overdid this activity when I was in primary school in the 1950s. Today, it's becoming a lost art. If taught too strictly or too snidely, it can make a child dislike English. But taught correctly, it's a valuable asset to understanding how grammar works.

Start with the simplest possible sentence: a noun and a verb. First explain to the child that a noun is a word often used as the subject of the sentence. A verb is an action word. The verb tells what's happening. The noun tells who or what is doing the action or to whom or what it's happening. You should also explain that though you can often *see* a noun—the boy, the girl, the table, you can only *see* a verb happening. *Run, walk, read* can be *seen* only while they're in action. That's why they're verbs.

Next, explain that grammar is the framework or skeleton of language. Grammar isn't something nasty that gives teachers the right to punish children. Grammar makes it possible for people to understand one another.

Here's an example of a simple sentence diagrammed:

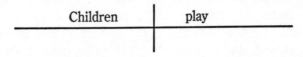

These two words form the simplest sentence, which has a noun and a verb. The first day you teach diagramming, you should make up a frame—a straight horizontal line with a straight vertical line through the center—and let the child help you make up a sentence with just a noun and a verb: "Dogs bark," "Birds fly," "Horses run," and "Cars go" are a few examples. Do this activity about 10 times, or until the child starts to become bored, so he or she understands the difference between a noun and a verb.

On the second day, introduce subjects and objects. The subject and the object are both nouns. But while the subject and the object are both nouns, they have different functions in the sentence.

Here's a sentence with a subject and an object:

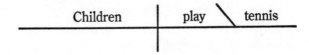

You should explain here that the subject, a noun, tells who is doing the action. The verb and the object together are called the *predicate* and tell what the subject is doing to whom or what. That's why the vertical line separates the subject from the predicate.

Next, add adjectives. You will remember that adjectives supply color, shape, size, speed, and other qualities that make a sentence more interesting. Here's what a fairly simple sentence should like in a diagram:

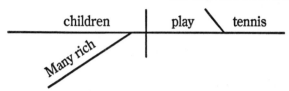

An adverb modifies a verb, an adjective, or another adverb much as an adjective modifies a noun. Adverbs often end in -*ly* in English, which makes many of them easy to spot. (If your student has studied French or German, you can explain that French adverbs end in -*ment* or -*mente* and German adverbs in -*lich*. One of the most important skills children learn when studying a foreign language is the ability to look at their own language analytically. This skill is probably why knowing a foreign language boosts SAT scores by 50 to 100 points in most cases.)

Here's our good old simple sentence decorated with an adverb as well as an adjective:

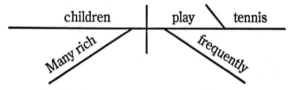

Next on the list is the prepositional phrase. The prepositional phrase is a cluster of words, without a verb, joined to the main sentence by a short word called a preposition.

"*With* my friends," "*at* the beach," "*in* the house," and "*by* the lake" are all prepositional phrases. In diagramming, the prepositional phrase is attached to the main sentence with the preposition as the link:

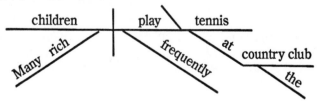

After that, there are articles—*a* and *an* are the indefinite articles, and *the* is the definite article. There are also conjunctions (joining words) specifically *and, or,* and *but,* which link clauses to a group of words that consists of a subject and a predicate. And that's about it for the major parts of speech and for diagramming.

The child can learn to diagram a sentence easily and without undue stress or strain in five or six lessons. After that, you should pull them aside for some diagramming during "together time" and explain to them what word goes where. Diagramming was widely disliked in the days of crabby old teachers who stressed them with a hickory stick; but if you can make it fun, it's a valid tool to better writing and more comprehensive advanced reading.

The proper age to begin diagramming is whenever your child has a complete confidence in reading and has begun to read for sheer enjoyment. If you start diagramming too early, you run the risk of turning off the child's interest in the written word by making everything into a pass-fail situation instead of a conduit of fun and information.

There's another way to study language structure that's enjoyable once diagramming has started and gives children a break from the routine. Invest in a set of see-through color markers with at least eight different colors, not including black or dark blue. Find some books with good, simple sentences, and photostat a couple of pages. Then go through the books, pick out sentences, and use a different color to mark each part of speech. You can use red for nouns, orange for adjectives, blue for verbs, light blue for adverbs (related to "blue" verbs), yellow for definite articles, and brown for indefinite articles. Or come up with your own color scheme—one that stresses the relationships between the words. Perhaps for this reason, it may be wise to use red-based colors for the subject part of the sentence and blue-based colors (including green) for the predicate part of the sentence. Seeing relationships is a big part of diagramming.

Once the child is reading fluently—and above all, spontaneously—you should probably do either diagramming or color lining two or three times a week for a few months; then come back to it for review about once a month. The whole point of the exercise isn't to get an "A" in diagramming. It's to teach the child a feeling for the structure of language that will make it easier for them to write and reason clearly later on. That's why it's best to hold off on formal grammar until the child is at least 8, better 9 or even 10 years old and has begun to form the capacity to understand abstraction. Few, if any, younger children have this ability, however quickly they learn. Concentrate on rote learning before the age of 9 or 10, and abstract learning (science, grammar, and math theory) later on. If you try to push the abstraction too early, you may produce a child who's frustrated, unhappy, and resists learning. On the other hand, if you delay the rote too long, you may produce a child with a reading or math problem.

The child who loves reading and understands most of what he or she reads, and who has mastered the times tables for multiplication and division completely and thoroughly before the age of 9 or 10, is basically failure-proofed in terms of basic education. It's appalling to consider how many students graduate from high school, and sometimes enter college, deficient in one or the other of these absolutely vital skills. Once they've been mastered, it's a pleasant surprise, both for parents and for child, to discover that the rest of it, while providing endless opportunities for shared fun and shared learning, is actually reasonably easy.

At this point, it's time to start introducing your student to experimental science.

About this time, some amusing and rather sloppy experiments punctuated my own home schooling. I wanted to show the kids what oxygen is. After the proper preparation, I had my lab set up on the kitchen table.

Here's what you will need for this experiment: a pie pan with an inch of water at the bottom, a large birthday candle, and a tempered glass jar an inch or two taller than the candle. Light the candle, keep it going, and then cover it quickly with the jar. You will see the candle flame flicker and then die. The level of the water inside the jar will suddenly rise about a quarter of the way up the side as water is mysteriously sucked up from the pie pan.

For those who skipped chemistry or general science in school, what has happened is that the flame has consumed all the available oxygen in the jar—about a quarter of the atmospheric air—and the water has risen to fill the space left by the oxygen consumed. (The remaining air in the jar is nitrogen and minor gases.)

You can buy books about other scientific experiments of this type with explanations. What you're doing, of course, is fostering a natural curiosity and a positive attitude toward science. The real study of chemistry requires a greater degree of mathematical sophistication than the average nine-year-old mind can hold.

If you look for them, opportunities to show the child practical science are everywhere. During summer vacation between what would have been third and fourth grade, Johnny told me he was tapped out on reading historical biographies and asked to read about technology for a while. I found good basic books by Herbert S. Zim in the children's library, and he devoured them two or three at a sitting. After reading the book about plumbing, he asked me where the stuff came out when you flushed the toilet or emptied the sink. One day while I had him with me in the car, running household errands for my wife on a day off, I took him to the regional sewage disposal plant, knocked at the office, and asked if they had a guided tour. To Johnny's utter amazement the engineer in charge of the operation graciously took 45 minutes of his schedule and showed us the whole plant. I told the man that while Johnny might not understand everything, he was very bright and literate for his age. We toured the settling tanks, the aeration tanks where the waste water is exposed to pumped air, the flow tanks where the water is exposed to ultraviolet light, and the sludge compactor and incinerator where the solid waste is burned at high temperatures. Johnny's comments astonished the engineer and showed that he understood more than either the engineer or I had expected.

And the high-tech equipment and the huge volume of water being processed absolutely fascinated him.

Best of all, he managed not to fall in.

Some experiments are not as potentially messy as this one, though they take longer. Johnny will never forget our indoor worm farm. While we were digging up topsoil for the vegetable garden at the Glen Rock Recycling Center, Johnny and I became involved in a discussion about where topsoil came from. He was doubtful when I explained to him that worm castings basically produced topsoil—the worms ate vegetation and recycled it into topsoil through ingestion, digestion, and egestion.

"You mean topsoil is worm poo-poo? And we put that stuff in our vegetable garden? Yuck!"

So we did an experiment. I found a clean apple juice bottle, and we filled it half-full of fresh lawn clippings and added six earthworms Johnny had rescued from puddles in the driveway after a rainstorm. The bottle was stored in a shady corner of the basement, and Johnny sprinkled it with a little water every few days. He also added some apple and banana peels destined for the compost heap.

"Everybody likes a little dessert—even worms," Johnny observed reasonably.

After three weeks, we formally inspected the bottle's contents. Most of the grass clippings had been reduced to mucky black topsoil, the level of vegetation in the bottle had been lowered about 60 percent due to being condensed—and the six worms had become six adults and eight slender baby worms.

"Good work, guys," Johnny said, as he returned them to the backyard compost, where they quickly squirmed into the soil.

During this time, needless to say, I had handed Johnny every book the children's library contained about worms, and several books on other agricultural topics. He apparently read them all with interest, because he could discourse on worms at great length: "Did you know that worms can have babies all by themselves because they're both male and female? Did you know that worms not only make topsoil, but keep the ground soft so plants can grow in it?" This experience was an introduction to invertebrates and agriculture that he never forgot.

Another activity both children enjoyed was watching the seed-to-plant process from spring to autumn in the garden. We prepared by getting some topsoil and the vegetable seeds we needed for our year's minicrop. I explained to the kids that some kinds of plants could be started as seedlings and later transplanted. Others, such as corn and root crops, couldn't be moved once they had sprouted. We started some tomatoes, lettuce, and cucumbers in trays. Shortly, the garden became more experimental. Johnny found a sprouted potato in the pantry and wanted to know what a potato looked like in the earth. We planted it. We had also been reading about American Indians and the importance of corn and beans in their cultures. We planted a few specimens as soon as it was warm enough.

During the unit on the American Civil War, I was struck by the many references to cotton and to how important it was to the economics and history of the South. I wrote to Bobby Horton, the Civil War balladeer whose tapes we used as background for our Civil War lessons, and he sent a whole ziplock bag full of cotton seeds. Finally, during some reading on the Russo-Japanese War, Emily was struck by the references to millet, the "poor man's crop" of Asia. I found some millet seeds in a bag of birdseed—the pale yellow ones that are tiny and round. We planted these seeds off to one side of the vegetable patch.

The neighbors may have thought that we had a very weird garden, but it was a garden rooted in history and blossoming into science. The children also derived tremendous fun out of rummaging gently through the foliage to find a cucumber for the supper salad, or a squash to be cooked with soup. When we had an excess of ripe squash or cucumbers, my wife dispatched Emily and Johnny to friends' houses with fresh vegetables as gifts. She received a lot of pleasure out of being able to help people out when she knew they might be short of money without insulting them by mentioning it. Emily and Johnny received a lot of pleasure out of the astonishment people showed when they examined the sizes of some of the vegetables. (We didn't show them any of the various crop failures.)

Another family activity that combined science and recreation was leaf walks. The children and I, sometimes with my wife, would arm ourselves with pocket guidebooks, plastic bags, sometimes a notebook and a magnifying glass, and — most important of all — comfortable shoes. Each season has its own blessing for nature walks, but the best season of all may be autumn. The children picked up one leaf from each type of tree, bagged it, and guessed what it might be. Later, at home, they examined the leaves, side by side with a guide-book to determine what type of leaves they were looking at. There are some places, called arboretums (living tree muse-ums) where the trees are marked and labeled, making identi-fication easier.

Winter nature walks were good for another quarry — animal tracks. There are also guidebooks for this activity, and you can make quite a game out of identifying which animal made the tracks found in the snow. A natural forest or a large park are the best places to do this exercise, but you can have a successful nature walk around a suburban neighborhood, or even a city lot, if you know what you're looking for. And in cities, the available botanical gardens compensate for the lack of forests and fields to some extent.

As the child's capacity for abstraction expands, and as their basic skills become so solid that they don't need routine drills as much as they did, you may want to move into the realm of theoretical mathematics, which isn't nearly as intimidating as it sounds.

You can also give the child a toehold on "pure" mathemat-ics or math theory, and a history lesson as well, by showing some of the mathematical discoveries of the Greeks and the

Arabs that led to modern mathematics.

Here's one lesson the child will probably pick up on with some excitement:

Have you ever wondered why square numbers are called *square?* Ask your child to try to guess.

Get some graph paper. Your child can use crayons for this exercise if he or she wants, but for our purposes we'll use different shapes.

Start off with a circle in the lower left square.

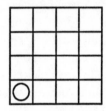

Then wrap the single circle with three split circles like this:

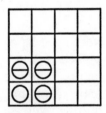

The sum of the circles (both simple and split) is 4, which is the first square number after 1. The child knows this answer from the times tables: 1 x 1 = 1, while 2 x 2 = 4.

Now wrap the first two squares with a third set of circles. This time, use circles with crosses inside them to show which set is which.

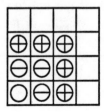

Now count up all the circles—simple, split, and crossed. You will find that the total is 9: 1 in the first set; 3 in the second set to make 4; and 5 in the third set you just made. The total is 9. And 9 is the third square number: 3 x 3 = 9.

Now wrap one more set around the first three. This time, use circles with x marks inside them to distinguish the new set from the other three.

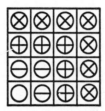

You will see that the sum of this new set and the three old sets is 16: 4 x 4 = 16. And the same holds true for 5 x 5, 6 x 6, 7 x 7, and so on. They are all *squares*.

The sets of wraparound square numbers are called *gnomons,* and they were reportedly discovered by Pythagoras, the legendary "father" of Greek mathematics, about 700 B.C. Children, especially the bright ones, get a tremendous lift out of exercises like this one. So did the ancient Greeks. The way the Greeks could keep making squares each time they multiplied a number by itself fascinated them. The fact that squares and their square roots (the numbers multiplied to make the squares) could be used to solve other problems in geometry also intrigued the Greeks. And if they fascinate your children, they're one step farther away from math phobia and one step farther down the road that leads to engineering or higher mathematics.

Another discovery, this one from the world of nature, is the set of Fibonacci numbers. These numbers were named after Leonardo da Pisa, an Italian mathematician of the later Middle Ages whose nickname was Fibonacci. Leonardo da Pisa discovered that numbers in the natural world often occur in a regular order: the numbers of the order are 1, 1, 2, 3, 5, 8, 13, 21, and so forth. Children can find these Fibonacci numbers in such places as the kernels of a pine cone or the petals radiating out from the center of certain flowers. You can keep predicting the next Fibonacci number by adding the two previous Fibonacci numbers:

$1 + 1 = 2$
$1 + 2 = 3$
$2 + 3 = 5$

And so on.

Ancient Greeks used the logic of mathematics to arrive at, among other things, the concept of one God and a belief in the immortality of the soul. People of the Middle Ages cited mathematical logic to confirm their faith as Christians in a universe that was governed by God's laws. This fact is worth pointing out to your child, just as it's worth pointing out that many great innovators in mathematics, including Copernicus, Kepler, Galileo, Newton, Leibnitz, Pascal, Lemaitre, Jeans, and Einstein were deeply religious men whose sense of God and spirituality pervaded their work. In later life, the child, now grown to a teenager, may encounter adults who attempt to pervert science into an attack against religion. The best way to insulate the child against this insidious influence is to give him or her a solid grounding in science and mathematics and explain that many of the greatest scientists, and in partic- ular those who were really benefactors of humankind like Louis Pasteur and Joseph Lister, were themselves deeply religious and followed their religious beliefs to make their greatest discoveries.

One of the best introductions to the math world beyond the basics is *Wonders of Mathematics,* by Rocco Feravolo. This book not only offers a history of mathematics, but describes how to use a sextant for navigating a ship and how to make a theodolite—a surveyor's tool used to calculate the heights and distances of objects. The book also contains arithmetic adventure games. Most larger children's libraries also contain books that offer simple introductions into probability, sets, number theory, and simple algebra and geometry. If one of the parents teaching at home is in any way mathematical or can learn to be mathematical, it's well worth setting aside some time to study these books side by side with your child.

The schools have abused the term *creative* to such an extent that as a professional writer I've come to wince when I hear it. In the first place, I know from hard experience just how difficult it is to earn a living in writing or any of the other arts. Those *creative* people who can actually find work in their chosen fields are probably the worst-paid people in America if you weigh their intelligence and effort against their real wages. And many, even those with genuine talent, can't find work at all. I think the schools do children a terrible disservice when they use *creativity* as a way to fill time and encourage a positive self-image instead of teaching the younger children a solid roster of basics and the teenagers a solid job skill.

Having said that, I must add that a good writing skill is a major asset in the academic world and the real world of jobs and professions that follows school and college. Yet, the expressive writing skills of young Americans are on a par with their abilities in math and foreign languages—which is to say, sad to tragic in most cases.

The key to good writing is good reading. The child who begins reading early and derives most of his or her information from books and good magazines has a lead that will never vanish over those who depend almost exclusively on television—unless, like the hare in Aesop's story of the turtle and the hare, the child goes to sleep in the middle of the race.

One of the best ways to teach writing is to encourage the child's efforts at storytelling. Some children will prefer printing longhand even after they learn to write cursive script. Others react well to typing; it's a sort of magic to make the letters appear. At first, you'll be pressed into service as an advisor whenever the child wants to "type a letter" to someone: "How do you spell this? How do you spell that?" Don't flee from this opportunity—embrace it. If you don't have a home typewriter or computer terminal that you would trust in a child's hands, even with supervision, you might want to invest in a child's typewriter, often available for around $25 in the better toy stores. Most children are naturally creative and will use this occasion to do various genuinely creative things—things that may be amusing from an adult's point of view, but which should be encouraged at all costs.

I remember when I was the editor-in-chief of a weekly newspaper, the children put out their own edition—*The Times of Mountain Falls*. Mountain Falls was a town that existed only for the purposes of the children's newspaper. The mayor's name was Fred Koster, and everybody else on the council, the police force, and the fire department was also named "Koster." The children seemed to have an intuitive understanding of the role that nepotism sometimes assumes in small-town politics, though Mountain Falls was probably the most nepotistic place on earth, as described in *The Times of Mountain Falls*.

Their little newspaper may have been written out longhand in block letters, with sketches for photos, but it was read. The writing, gently critiqued and subtly encouraged, gave both kids a chance to practice their grammar, spelling, punctuation, and news style. The two "Mountain Falls" editors quickly moved from the theoretical to the practical. During peak work loads when I had to go into the office over the weekend, I took them with me. Johnny, who was then about 7, ran errands around the office; Emily, then 11, was pressed into service as a relief typesetter. So while my editorial assistant, Dawn Esposito, rested her eyes from several hours of high-speed word processing, Emily sat down in her place and typeset a number of stories into the VDT, which later turned up in print before 36,000 readers, who probably would have been surprised to know that the "journalist" who produced the story from a press release was 11 years old.

Apprenticeship programs at a weekly newspaper aren't practical for everybody. But there are writing experiences that every child can have. For a start, you can have your child write a real thank-you note each time they receive a present or an invitation. The experience of sending and receiving letters is one that most children look forward to.

Some children react with great pride to having overseas pen pals—a great asset in the study of foreign languages and world cultures later in education. You can often pick up addresses through international pen pal clubs, foreign embassies or consulates. Or you can try something a little less conventional. After we had watched a TV news show about how the new Soviet policy had restored freedom of religious belief and made way for the unification of Germany and greater freedom for Poland and Hungary, our family discussed whether or not the reforms were real. The kids and I did some research. We talked to people who had friends and relatives living in the affected nations. The mother of Emily's East German pen pal family (shortly to become a West German pen pal family, and eventually just a German pen pal family) reported that most of what we read in the newspapers was true. Freedom was really returning to Eastern Europe. Our family driver—the Hungarian refugee whom I asked for by name when I needed an airport limo ride—said the same. He had been back to Hungary for the first time since 1956, after leaving one jump ahead of the Russian tanks, and he definitely wasn't soft on Communism or unduly fond of the Russians as a people. But his report was that many basic freedoms actually had been restored.

Taking pen in hand—actually, by this time, she had learned to type so she took typewriter in hand—Emily wrote a letter to Soviet President Mikhail Gorbachev, praising him for his reforms and urging him to keep up the good work and ensure complete freedom of religion in a nation that had promulgated state atheism for 60 years.

In a P.S., she asked if the censor who read the letter knew of any young girls in the Soviet Union who wanted to write to a young girl in the United States. The letter, plastered with about a dozen colorful stamps, was duly dispatched to: Premier Mikhail Gorbachev, The Kremlin, Moscow, USSR/CCCP. After a few days, we forgot we had ever sent it.

Six months later, an airmail letter with a Soviet postmark

showed up addressed to Emily Koster. Inside, Emily found a letter from her new Soviet pen pal, Sonya. There was one slight problem. Sonya wrote her return address in Cyrillic cursive script, which nobody in our family could either read or plausibly duplicate. Consternation arose as we puzzled on how to send a response back to an address nobody could read. After some fretting, Emily arrived at the obvious solution: Make a high-resolution photostatic copy of the Cyrillic cursive return address and paste it onto the envelope. The idea worked, because Sonya received our letter and a regular correspondence began.

A hidden advantage in seeking overseas pen pals for your students goes beyond the ability to write letters in English, or even to reinforce the importance of learning other languages. Children in other countries don't go to class to show off their clothes or make fun of the teachers. Academics are taken very seriously in the rest of the world. Some of this attitude by a foreign pen pal may rub off.

The formal writing exercise should come after the child has already begun to enjoy writing for fun. Making writing into an unwanted chore does more harm than good.

One of our best tools for the formal home study writing exercise proved to be *The Story of a Castle,* an illustrated book by John S. Goodall (MacMillan). *Illustrated* is the key, because the whole book consists of an artist's color illustrations of an English castle from Norman times in the A.D. 1100s to the 1970s. There are no words whatsoever, except in the introductory notes. When Emily first discovered the book I initially balked at paying out good money for a book with no reading in it, but I saw a purpose that turned out to make the book well worth the price.

Our first attempt at a formal writing exercise was to set the book down and open it to one double-page spread showing the Roundheads (supporters of Parliament) attacking a castle defended by the Cavaliers (supporters of King Charles I) in the 1640s. Emily and Johnny each sat at a clear, empty table, armed with a lined spiral notebook and a pen. They had

a half hour, if necessary, to write anything they wanted to
about what was happening in the picture and the double-page
spread on the next page, which showed the victorious Roundheads looting the castle.

Here's how Johnny described it:

*The round heads came to collect the cavaliers taxes. The cava-
liers did not want to pay the taxes so they had a fight. Finally the
round heads won and took the cavaliers goods.*

Emily saw the scene somewhat differently:

*"Build a blockade" commanded Richard the leader of the
King's Cavaliers. "The roundheads will be upon us soon."*

*The women gasped and quaked with fear and held their chil-
dren to their bosoms. "It is not for our lives that we fear," one
cried, "it is for the lives of our children. Cromwell's men will
show no mercy to neither women nor child."*

"Have faith," her husband replied.

*"Load your muskets," ordered the 2nd-in-command. "The
roundheads are storming up the hill."*

*"Defend your country, your women, and children" another
cried.*

*Dead silence settled over the room as the soldiers approached
the castle.*

*Suddenly musket fire rang out in the room as the roundheads
bit the dirt. Pictures of noble ancestors were torn off the wall, or
placed askew; Curtains ripped and wood broke as women's
screams and children's cries filled the air. The men fought
bravely, but soon all the cavaliers and their wives and children
had perished.*

*Dead bodies lay everywhere, with grotesque bullet wounds and
swords in them.*

*The roundheads sacked the castle taking all valuables, once
the prized possessions of the dead bodies on the ground, who had
been sent up to a better place.*

I should point out that neither Emily, at 13, nor Johnny, at
9 going on 10, was exactly a stranger to the English Civil
War. Both of them had read *The Flight and Adventures of
Charles II,* by Charles Norman, one of the most readable and

exciting of all Landmark books. Both had read *Oliver Cromwell*, by Amanda Purvis (Wayland), and both had read the portion of English history that revolved around the conflict between the King and Parliament in *The Story of Britain*, by R. J. Unstead, a superb introduction to the drama and color of British history for older children or younger teens. They had also seen the film *Cromwell* with Richard Harris and Alec Guinness. Emily, in addition, had read the Wayland books on James I, by David Walter, and on Charles II, by Michael Gibson, and Clifford Lindsey Alderman's excellent *Death to the King*, (Julian Messner), the story of the English Civil War.

Both Emily and Johnny had also read the Illustrated Children's Classic version of *The Three Musketeers*, which is set in the same general era and has fictionalized versions of some of the real characters who played their parts in the downfall of Charles I. They had also read all three of Burke Wilkinson's wonderful books on the French kings of the era: *The Helmet of Navarre* (about Henri IV), *Cardinal in Armor* (about Armand de Richelieu), and *Young Louis XIV*, in which we learn that, yes, there really was a Captain D'Artagnan of the King's Musketeers.

The key to good writing—and good spelling—is good reading, and plenty of it.

The key to good editing, on the other hand, is not to jump all over the child's first efforts and make him or her permanently pencil shy. A flashed instinct on the part of somebody who had never suffered under bad editors, as was my experience in my early newspaper work, would have been to critique Johnny's and Emily's stories against some lofty and unattainable goal. By these standards, Johnny's story would have been much too short and not nearly vivid enough. Emily's would have been too wordy and too full of clichés.

That's a terrible way to edit, especially when you're dealing with bright and sensitive children who are just feeling their way.

The good qualities about Johnny's story: It was terse; it was factual; it gave a plausible explanation of why the battle shown in the picture took place; and the spelling was quite good considering his age. The bad point was that it was so good we wanted to read more of it. This reponse is the kind of attitude, on the part of a critic, that encourages children to feel confidence in themselves and to enjoy writing—and to want to do better at it through constant and voluntary practice.

Emily proved even easier to critique. I let her read the story back a few days later, and she remarked:

"Some of the dialogue sounds pretty phony, doesn't it?"

In terms of correction, the best way to teach the child how to spell, punctuate, and organize is the "good guy/bad guy" approach. Find somebody else's bad example for your child's first efforts to correct bad spelling or to teach that child how to capitalize and punctuate.

One of the best ways I found to teach capitalization was to use press releases that some people insisted on sending me with every letter capitalized. Journalists encounter these diamonds-in-the-rough routinely. Sit the child down, and tell him or her to insert instructions for proper capitalization. (In proofreader's markings, three lines are placed under the letter to be capitalized. In case you've forgotten, the words you must capitalize are the first word of each sentence; the names of individual people, towns, cities, and countries; names given as part of a title; Mayor John Smith, Board of Education President Linda Stuart, Chief of Police Neil Finn; titles of books, movies, and businesses; and types of ships, airplanes, cars, and trucks. A zany fad is abroad in the land—at least among some people who send press releases to smaller newspapers—to capitalize every noun. Resist it. It immediately denotes the writer is uneducated, no matter how well he or she spells or punctuates. But don't let this warning insult you. I continually catch some of the younger reporters who work for me capitalizing every noun, as if they were writing in German. And some of them are people in their middle 20s with two college degrees.)

Examples of really bad writing to be criticized and improved by the child should come, initially, from anonymous outsiders the child does not know. They are the "bad guys." But you don't teach the children to hate, despise, or even ridicule these anonymous "bad guys"—teaching children contempt for the less fortunate is a bad and ugly idea. What you teach them is not to make the same mistakes.

Once they've learned to spot mistakes in other (anonymous) people's writing, they can better improve their own. One thing I told them to make writing more fun is to talk to themselves. Writers, whether professional or amateur, have the right to talk to themselves without being called "crazy," as in that old catch phrase of my own childhood: "Only crazy people talk to themselves." In fact, all good writers appear to talk to themselves at least mentally, trying out sentences, phrases, titles, voicing them to catch the ring of true metal or detect the clink and clank of verbal dross. You can't be a writer unless you love the language and rehearse it, more or less constantly. This is why the single great key to good writing is good reading, reading the best books early and often. In writing, as in life, a pound of good example is a lot easier to digest and assimilate than an ounce of even the most constructive criticism—and the bad effects of hostile criticism are enormous and poisonous.

The upkeep on the foreign language programs is worth some consideration as well. If your child began studying French, German, Spanish, or Italian by the age of 6, your 10-year-old probably has a better grasp on the fundamentals of the language and a larger functional vocabulary than many students who have taken a year or two of the language in high school. Your only problem now is to bridge the three or four years until the child is ready to turn the foreign language into an easy "A" and a major credential for college admission or job applications.

Listening to records in foreign languages was one of the best ways we found to make this bridge. Emily came across these records naturally. Her love of opera made it almost impossible to pry her away from the stereo and the libretto that contained the German-English, Italian-English, or French-English texts.

Johnny was a more difficult case. Somebody must have told him that red-blooded American he-men were supposed to *hate* opera. Getting him to sit still was a real test of wills. So we had to be selective. For a German-language opera, we saddled him primarily with *The Magic Flute,* by Mozart. The German text is extremely simple, since it was written for a cosmopolitan Viennese audience whose first language may not have been German, and the characters are simple embodiments of basic virtues and vices. In fact, if it were not for the music, *The Magic Flute* would be almost an operatic cartoon. Johnny had a panpipe, and we encouraged him to play it, along with Pagageno, the comic birdcatcher, who functions as the plot's clown figure. Johnny actually enjoyed this opera enough to sing along in spots. Since Papageno is a baritone part and Johnny was a boy soprano, the results weren't exactly what Mozart had intended, especially since Johnny tried to shift his voice into the baritone range. He sounded something like a bullfrog who sang off key. Emily, on the other hand, could hit every note of the Queen of the Night's highest arias and did so, which sometimes prompted Johnny to clap both hands over his ears and grimace. No eardrums were broken, but several battles of the critics were carried on at a decibel level somewhat above the recording.

For French opera, we started with Jacques Offenbach's *The Grand Dutchess of Gerolstein,* a comic operetta. Emily understood that several of the scenes were satires on serious grand operas from Offenbach's own day, notably the conspiracy scene in *Les Huguenots,* by Meyerbeer, and the song of the King of Thule from *Faust,* by Gounod. These operas were two of Emily's favorite serious operas, but she had cut her teeth on *The Grand Dutchess* and didn't take umbrage. I was glad to see that listening to the opera records and following the words had become a part of the family's regular evening schedule, several nights a week and every Saturday and Sunday evening, Johnny dropped his pose of being a he-man opera-hater and began to relate to the characters and the music.

Children have a great sense of mischief, and it was hard for Johnny not to enjoy some of the tales of Offenbach: A French composer (he was actually a Jewish German converted to Catholicism by a wife who was English and Spanish) he managed to write the music that everyone thinks of as "typically French," and to popularize the cancan. His operettas satirize all the foibles, frauds, and failures of an era that was at once glittering, profoundly important, and dismal. The beauty of his music, however light, is of a charm that can't be ignored. Richard Wagner, the ultimate heavy composer, once told Pierre Renoir, who was painting his portrait, that he hated Offenbach for his popularity in Paris at a time when he himself was ignored and living in dire poverty. Renoir indignantly replied that he had never missed an Offenbach first night when he could afford one and loved his music. Wagner then ruefully replied that it was "leetle" music, but beautiful, and that if Offenbach hadn't been preoccupied with turning out first-night smashes, he could have been another Mozart. When you tell your child that Offenbach was also the composer of "The Marines' Hymn," the child has a perspective on the world of culture that fascinates but doesn't intimidate. It's a link that the child will find some way to relate to—light music, heavy music, Impressionist art, and the Marines!

That's a big part of your child's continuing education— learning to carry on conversations on adult subjects. Have you ever considered how appalled college professors must be to contemplate teaching European history to students who have never heard of Offenbach, Renoir, or Wagner—though they may have heard of the Marines? And then imagine how glad they will be to talk with your children.

Learning goes on forever. Once your students have mastered the basics—whether through a full home schooling program or through supplemental home education augmented by the school program—they have just started on an adventure of a lifetime.

Whether you're schooling your child at home or supplementing his or her education with a few hours a day or a few hours a week of home teaching, there are a few ways to make sure that your student stays on top academically.

1. Children should be encouraged to read constantly, for information and for pleasure. Conversations, field trips, or even the use of the TV to show feature films or documentaries can stimulate this reading. But there is no substitute for books.

2. Whether or not students are enrolled in school math classes, they should spend about 15 minutes a day on math drills featuring addition, subtraction, multiplication, and division, and expand as far as you can take them on your own or with the help of store-bought texts. Even schools that are otherwise effective usually don't provide enough drill in math basics, probably because some of the students and their parents don't want them to. Don't "go with the crowd" on this one—it's too important.

3. Try to focus whatever TV you let the child watch around shows that are genuinely educational as opposed to those that are popular with the student's peers. The educational shows on PBS, documentaries, and feature films with historical settings are no substitute for reading, but they *are* far superior to gossipy talk shows, situation comedies, and cheap violent cartoons. The real point, however, is to use these shows as a lead-in to reading books on the topic or to family discussions that encourage the child to use an encyclopedia or read newspapers and magazines to learn more.

4. Try to gear the "quality time" you spend with your family away from shopping, theme parks, and even from sports events toward those destinations that provide real educational opportunities: museums, zoos, botanical gardens, and industrial sites if tours are offered. You may not believe this statement, but the child who becomes a rabid "sports nut" is often more interested in pleasing his or her parent than he or she is in the sport. And if the child is a spectator rather than a player, the value either in physical

or mental terms is close to zero.

There's a book called *Treasures of America,* published by *Reader's Digest,* that lists thousands of day-trip or weekend destinations on a region-by-region basis, besides containing a brief and readable course in the art and architecture found in various parts of the United States. Taking a couple of Saturdays or Sundays per month to visit some of these sites, even the ones that are just a short distance from your own home, will offer your children ready-made discoveries in history and culture that will stimulate reading and a better understanding of what's read. This way, education keeps expanding; and this way, children grow into adults who know how to think, appreciate, and keep learning all their lives.

Children learn what they see, and not just what you tell them. If you nag them about the education they aren't getting and then turn back to the TV, they'll assume you really don't care either. But parents who play an active role in their child's education, whether as a full-time home teacher or a supplemental teacher who studies with the child a few hours a day or a few hours a week, are showing the child just how important education really is in terms that can't be misunderstood. That's probably why home schooling, either on a part-time or full-time basis, produces such superb results for almost everyone who tries it. Whether you're trying to produce a multilingual honor student or just making sure that your child doesn't miss out on the basics while there's still time to learn them, you'll find that learning at home is an experience that teaches the whole family lessons in love.

Teaching Helps

SUPPLEMENTAL SYLLABUS

This syllabus is intended for the busiest of parents. The syllabus assumes that the child is in a regular school program and aims at providing a solid basis for further academic progress, though not the kind of advanced academic enrichment described in several chapters.

Ages Two to Four

You should spend 15 to 30 minutes, once or twice a day, reading beside the child from books with attractive pictures and simple stories.

The child should also be encouraged to watch "Sesame Street" on a regular basis, once or possibly even twice a day.

Ages Four to Five

You should sit beside the child, teach the letters of the alphabet and the numbers 1 to 10 by drawing them, and encourage him or her to match words to pictures in children's books. By the age of five, after two or three years of "Sesame Street" and side-by-side reading, the child should be making attempts to read spontaneously. Further details about teaching basic reading are available in the chapter on how to teach reading.

Ages Five to Six

You should spend 10 minutes teaching the child to write and read basic words, as described in the chapter on teaching children how to read. You and your child should then spend 20 to 30 minutes reading side by side, with you filling in only those words the child doesn't know. Use the same four or five books over until the child has memorized the stories, then change. The child should spend the last 10 to 15 minutes of the lesson time counting, naming numbers, and learning how to add and subtract with the aid of a counting frame or small visible objects like coins or checkers, as described in the chapter on how to teach math.

Ages Six to Seven
The child should now be reading fluently and, with a little encouragement, voluntarily. You may cut back side-by-side reading to about 15 minutes with more difficult material. The remaining 45 minutes should be divided into 15 minutes of free reading of supervised material at the child's own level — *not* at the school's level, which will be far below the child's, 15 minutes of doing math problems together, and 15 minutes of writing out the answers to the times tables, after you've explained what times tables are and why they are important.

Ages Seven through Eight
With some reinforcement, the child should now know the times tables completely and be able to handle the four basic functions of math. You should make up regular lessons with the four basic functions and simple word problems, and use about half an hour to encourage the child to do these lessons and to correct them. You should spend 15 minutes either reading beside the child or discussing what the child has read. The use of VCR films to encourage the child to read classic children's stories or children's biographies, as discussed in the chapters on television and the humanities programs, is remarkably effective with children once they become voluntary readers. (Note that movie watching doesn't count as part of the regular one hour of class. You may want to watch the movie with the child over the weekend and set aside time during each hour for reading the book.)

Ages Eight through Ten
At this point, you will want to spend most of your hour per day assigning and grading your child's math lessons and discussing the books they're reading. In math, the child should be doing percentages, fractions, and the other skills described in the last chapter of the book. You may also want to buy books on math or take them out of libraries to create enriched lessons.

ADVANCED SUPPLEMENTAL SYLLABUS
This advanced supplemental syllabus assumes you and your spouse, separately or together, can put together two hours a day when one or both of you can be with the child. This time allows not only an enriched and reinforced grounding in the basics but a chance to offer a foreign language and some other academically advanced material.

Ages Two to Four
The syllabus here is basically the same, and it's probably not necessary to spend more than an hour reading and counting with the child if he or she also watches "Sesame Street" and other educational television.

Ages Four to Five
You should sit beside the child and read stories from illustrated books but should limit the lesson's length only by the child's apparent attention span. In practical terms, this means the lesson can be prolonged until the child becomes cranky or sleepy, but not beyond this point.

The child should *never* come to think of early lessons as a form of punishment. Begin each lesson with 15 minutes of naming numbers and counting, then proceed with the reading and naming of letters and words until the child becomes satiated with the exercise. This exercise will usually consume far less than two hours allotted, but the child's ability to read will expand much faster than if the lessons last only 15 to 30 minutes.

Ages Five to Six

You should now begin to teach the child to write basic words with the methods described in the chapter on how to teach reading. The math lessons may be as much as 30 minutes, including counting with the counting frame or solid objects, and writing out the times tables.

Ages Six to Seven

With the additional reading possible in this advanced syllabus, the child should now have progressed to fluent and voluntary reading of children's stories and easy juvenile biographies from the "Easy Reader" section of the children's library. The extra time for math should be pointing the child toward memorization of the times tables.

At this point, you may use 30 minutes of the allotted two hours to start teaching a foreign language, as described in the chapter on teaching foreign languages (chap. 3). (The child will need to have a reasonable ability to read simple English before you can begin to study and learn French or one of the other languages, especially if you don't speak the language yourself.) You can use the books and methods described in the text.

Ages Seven to Eight

By this age, the two-hour syllabus should consist of about 15 minutes of side-by-side reading, covering material the child might not tackle alone, 30 minutes of side-by-side foreign-language study (you may learn as much as the child does if you both put your minds to it), and 15 minutes of teaching the child to print or write basic words. The second hour should consist of 15 minutes of doing math with the child, a half hour of letting the child do structured math lessons (see the text), and 15 minutes of correcting, in which you explain what the child is doing wrong while fulsomely praising his or her correct answers. At this point, constant drill on the times tables should be about half the math lesson until the child knows them perfectly.

Ages Eight to Ten

At this point, the child should know the whole roster of math skills perfectly, from addition and subtraction through the times tables, division, and problems with decimals and fractions. Check math enrichment in the last chapter and look up others in books. You can also find books in stationery stores on graded math lessons. The child should do a series of these lessons, probably about two years ahead of his or her own chronological age. Try to spot any areas with which the child has trouble and provide encouragement and reinforcement, but without harshness or negative criticism.

Your foreign language lessons, other than supervised reading by the child, may now consist of games like those described in the text, or of listening to audio tapes or, better yet, to classical or popular music in that language, with a dual-language libretto. By this time also, you should have acquired several storybooks and a Bible in the language you're teaching, and the child should do repetitious reading of folk or fairy tales and Bible stories until they can read the individual stories easily.

In terms of English, formal lessons may now be limited to writing instruction, as described in the text, and discussion of the books the child is reading. In practice, once the child has become a fluent reader, the parent should set aside at least an hour a day when the child is to read, not necessarily beside the parent, but with no access to TV or rock music. Good videotapes should supplement the reading program to stimulate the child's interest in specific stories, personalities, and eras of history, as described in the chapters on television and the humanities program.

It's also a good idea, if possible, to set aside one weekend per month for an inexpensive family field trip to a museum, historic home, nature center, or some other point of interest, with readings before and after the expedition.

HOME SCHOOL SYLLABUS

While home schooling isn't practical for a vast number of

American families due to the need for two incomes and the increase in single-parent families, it's a growing movement. The number of U.S. home schoolers reached 500,000 in 1990, a tenfold increase over 10 years. For those dedicated and fortunate parents who wish to try home schooling, the general syllabus my wife and I used was something along these lines.

Ages Two through Four
The child should watch "Sesame Street" and other educational programs for about two hours a day. Beginning before the age of three, one parent should read to the child for 15 to 30 minutes and teach counting and numbers 10 to 15 minutes. The child also should accompany the adult or adults virtually everywhere except to work.

Ages Four to Five
The child begins formal lessons in reading and simple math around the age of four. This activity consists of recognizing short words and sounding out longer ones; writing letters of the alphabet, numbers, and simple words; and recognizing mathematical problems of addition and subtraction by using the counting frame, coins, checkers, or toys.

Ages Five to Six
The child begins independent reading of children's stories, with some additional reading side by side to encourage the child to attempt difficult material. Math lessons consist of regular problems in addition and subtraction and filling out the answers to the times tables. Other incentives to reading include following the words to English-language folk songs, Victorian ballads, and Gilbert and Sullivan songs while listening to the music and singing on records.

Ages Six to Seven
Formal training in foreign languages begins, at first, with 15 minutes per day of side-by-side instruction in each of two

languages, French and German. At this point, most lessons have been formalized to the point where they could be carried out without direct side-by-side supervision. The schedule is:

Math: 45 minutes per day—30 minutes worth of computation problems and 15 minutes to fill in the answers for the entire times table from memory.

French: 45 minutes per day—15 minutes of side-by-side reading and 30 minutes of review reading of material already covered.

German: 45 minutes—15 minutes of side-by-side reading and 30 minutes of review reading of material already covered.

English/History/Geography: two hours of thematic reading in children's books about historical figures, eras, or events, and about other cultures and countries.

Penmanship: 15 minutes a day copying words and letters; later, 15 to 30 minutes writing to friends and pen pals or describing events witnessed, places visited, or scenes from books.

Piano: 30 minutes of practice a day.

Athletics: one hour of outdoor exercise playing with other children or doing exercises under parental supervision. The children also should accompany parents on shopping trips and visits that are conducted on foot for most distances under half a mile.

During the temperate or summer months, the period of outdoor exercise and recreation should be expanded on Saturdays and Sundays for most of the afternoon. The children are not allowed to play outside during the hours when other children are at school, however, except during brief breaks after especially difficult lessons.

Ages Eight through Ten
The expanding abilities of the child to concentrate and handle more difficult material lead to lessons of greater breadth and depth.

Math: 60 minutes per day—15 minutes of side-by-side instruction in such skills as computing the area of triangles and the volumes of pyramids, cones, and spheres, reading angles with a protractor, and using known angles to find unknown ones. The remaining 45 minutes should consist of math lessons that cover everything from the most basic arithmetic through multiplication to four or five places, division of long numbers and fractions, calculating percentages, averages, constants and variables, and simple algebra, geometry, and the extremely basic forms of trigonometry and calculus. The children also should hone their skills by calling off the amount of change during shopping expeditions, usually before the cashier and register do.

French: One hour—15 minutes of side-by-side exploratory reading, 15 minutes of independent review reading, and 30 minutes listening to one record of an opera with the dual-language libretto.

German: One hour—15 minutes of side-by-side exploratory reading, 15 minutes of independent review reading, and 30 minutes of listening to one record of an opera with the dual-language libretto.

English/History/Geography: three hours of thematic reading. This reading could range from a complete Landmark or Signature book to several chapters of a more difficult book. Watching videotapes of the era under study should encourage reading, but should not count as "class time," and it should be done at night or on weekends.

Penmanship/Writing: The child is encouraged to spend at least a half hour a day either writing to pen pals, local friends, or relatives, filling out a diary, or describing scenes from books, movies, operas, or field trips.

Piano: 30 minutes of practice per day, one formal 45-minute lesson per week.

Athletics: The children are allowed to leave the house as soon as the other children in the neighborhood return from school so they can enjoy playing with their friends. They should be told they can play outside for a maximum of one hour unless they have finished all their lessons. If all formal lessons are complete, they can play outside until suppertime, and return for additional free time until sunset during the longer months with sunlight. Evenings are spent on "free reading" — anything wholesome, including children's mysteries, folk stories, and children's magazines — or on games with parents, ranging from *Chutes and Ladders* to checkers and chess. Television is permitted if the shows are educational or if they feature films with historical or geographical settings and a low threshhold of violence and sexuality.

By sticking to this schedule, with lapses only for sickness, family emergencies, or special field trips, we produced two children who achieved top scores in the California Achievement Tests without any cramming, while acquiring full childhood literacy in three or four foreign languages. (My daughter later added Italian and Spanish, and my son, a better mechanic, mathematician, and draftsman than his sister but less of a linguist, is now adding Italian and will probably add Spanish later.)

Curriculum Resources

ENGLISH LANGUAGE RESOURCES
Children love receiving their own personal magazines in the mailbox. Whether your child is a full-time home schooler or a student at a public or religious school with supplemental teaching on your part, you will almost certainly want to sign your child or children up for at least one subscription.

For Children of all Ages
Highlights for Children, a handsome magazine with cheery illustrations, is committed to constructive stories without violence or horror. Each issue contains stories at several levels, from beginning reader to preteen.
Highlights for Children
Dept. CA, PO Box 269
Columbus, OH 43216-0269

Ladybug, a new release from the publishers of *Cricket,* aims at younger children than *Cricket,* which is geared to preteens in upper elementary school.
Ladybug
PO Box 5843
Boulder, CO 80321-8343

Children's Better Health Institute publishes a whole family of children's magazines geared to wholesome reading and the promotion of healthy nutrition, good exercise, and sanitation.

These magazines are: *Stork* (ages 1–3), *Turtle* (ages 2–5), *Humpty Dumpty* (ages 4–6), *Children's Playmate* (ages 5–7), *Jack and Jill* (ages 6–8), and *Children's Digest* (ages 8–10). These magazines may be ordered—based on reading level, which should be higher than actual age for home schooled or supplemented students—from:
Children's Better Health Institute
PO Box 7133
Red Oak, IA 51591-2133

Cricket is often described as *"The New Yorker* of children's magazines." Geared toward the preteenaged reader, *Cricket* includes classic and original children's stories with superb illustrations and painless but effective vocabulary-building margin notes. I strongly recommend it for children who already know how to read fluently but aren't quite ready for adult publications.
Cricket, The Magazine for Children
Box 52947
Boulder CO 80321-2947

Ranger Rick is a children's magazine of geography and natural sciences published by the National Wildlife Federation. Stories with talking animals, offering genuine facts about nature, alternate with realistic photo features displaying extraordinary photographs.
Ranger Rick
National Wildlife Federation
1412 Sixteenth Street N.W.
Washington, D.C. 20036-9967

Other Resources
The Metropolitan Museum of Art in New York City produces dozens of books on all aspects of art and art history. Those people who can't get to New York City can shop by mail through catalogs that arrive at regular intervals and may be requested with or without making purchases. Besides books,

the museum offers reproductions of art objects, posters, greeting cards, and video tapes of lectures on a wide range of subjects.
The Metropolitan Museum of Art
255 Gracie Station
New York, NY 10028

The Metropolitan Opera in New York City has an extensive package of materials that can be used to educate children about opera, which, incidentally, is an excellent way to enliven a foreign-language program in French, German, or Italian. Also available are books and operas on video tapes, recordings, cassette tapes, and compact discs. Catalogs may be requested by writing to:
The Metropolitan Opera Guild
1865 Broadway
New York, NY 10023

Rand McNally publishes a catalog that offers a variety of globes, maps, and books about geography. The catalog offers material from the National Geographic Society for children as well.
Rand McNally
Publishing Direct Mail
PO Box 1697
Skokie, IL 60076-8697

Dover Publications produces reprints of classic books that have gone out of print, as well as some modern books. The extensive line of educational material available ranges from instruction tapes in foreign languages to cutout and coloring books about the history of costume and architecture to world classics, some of them in the original languages.
Dover Publications
31 East 2nd Street
Mineola, NY 11501

Special Interest Video offers a varied selection of instructional and documentary videotapes as well as some classic and contemporary films.
Special Interest Video
475 Oberlin Avenue South
CN 2112
Lakewood, NJ 08701-1062

FOREIGN LANGUAGE RESOURCES
Parents who decide to follow the instructions in this book and introduce their children to one or more foreign languages may encounter problems once they go beyond the two basic teaching books I recommend: *See It and Say It...* (Signet) and *Fun with...* (Little, Brown) are available in French, German, Italian, and Spanish. Some of the books are out of print, but most larger children's libraries will have a copy.

There is a wealth of supplemental material available for home teaching or supplemental teaching of foreign languages, especially of French. Here are some of the resources I have encountered.

International Linguistics Corporation
3505 E. Red Bridge Road
Kansas City, MO 64137
Complete children's language courses, by picture/language association, are available in French, German, Spanish, Chinese, and Russian.

Audio Forum
Room 1422
96 Broad Street
Guilford, CT 06437
(1-800-243-1234)
Foreign language cassettes for children and adults, including the "Springboard" and "Storybridges" series, offer familiar stories sprinkled with foreign words. Ask for the free catalog, and see what you can use.

Librairie De France
610 5th Avenue
New York, NY 10020
212-581-8810

This store carries a full line of instructional material to teach French to children, plus French literary classics and children's books. They will do business by mail if you can't get to New York City. Ask for Marie-Claude.

French Institute—Alliance Francaise
22 E. 60th Street
New York, NY 10022
212-355-6100

An organization that specializes in teaching French to Americans and promoting French culture in the United States.

Schoenhof's Foreign Books
76A Mt. Auburn Street
Cambridge, MA 02138
617-547-8855

A large selection of books in French, Spanish, German, and Italian, including children's books.

MISCELLANEOUS RESOURCES

Linda Russell, the colonial balladeer, and Bobby Horton, who specializes in popular music of the Civil War era, North and South, are mentioned in the chapter on bringing field trips to life. While their records or tapes may be available at some historic sites and speciality shops, they probably won't be found in the typical record store. The best thing to do is to write to them at their regular business addresses if you want your children to sample authentic colonial or Civil War music at home or on the car tape deck going to a museum or re-enactment.

Linda Russell
250 W. 99th St. Apt. 8C
New York, NY 10025

Bobby Horton
5245 Beacon Dr.
Birmingham, AL 35210